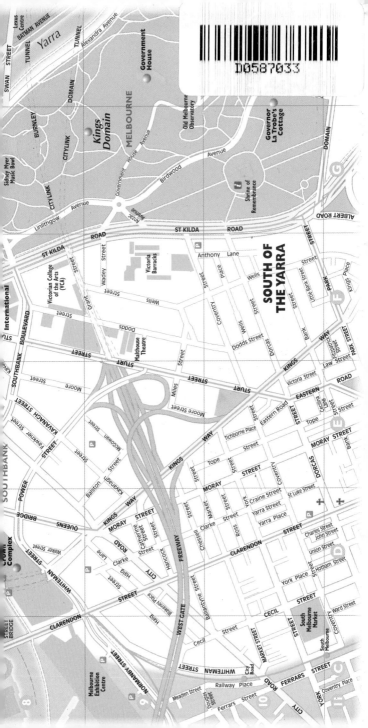

CITYPACK TOP 25
Melbourne

ROD RITCHIE
ADDITIONAL WRITING BY JULIE WALKDEN

If you have any comments
or suggestions for this guide
you can contact the editor at
Citypack@theAA.com

AA Publishing
Find out more about AA Publishing and the wide
range of services the AA provides by visiting our
website at www.theAA.com/travel

How to Use This Book

KEY TO SYMBOLS

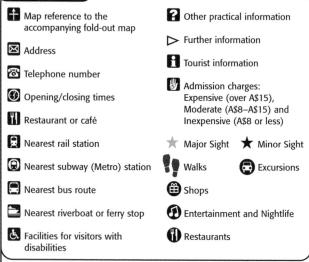

✚ Map reference to the accompanying fold-out map

✉ Address

☎ Telephone number

🕐 Opening/closing times

🍴 Restaurant or café

🚆 Nearest rail station

Ⓜ Nearest subway (Metro) station

🚌 Nearest bus route

⛴ Nearest riverboat or ferry stop

♿ Facilities for visitors with disabilities

❓ Other practical information

▷ Further information

ℹ Tourist information

✋ Admission charges: Expensive (over A$15), Moderate (A$8–A$15) and Inexpensive (A$8 or less)

⭐ Major Sight   ★ Minor Sight

👣 Walks   🚌 Excursions

🎁 Shops

🎵 Entertainment and Nightlife

🍴 Restaurants

This guide is divided into four sections

• **Essential Melbourne:** An introduction to the city and tips on making the most of your stay.

• **Melbourne by Area:** We've broken the city into six areas, and recommended the best sights, shops, entertainment venues, nightlife and restaurants in each one. Suggested walks help you to explore on foot.

• **Where to Stay:** The best hotels, whether you're looking for luxury, budget or something in between.

• **Need to Know:** The info you need to make your trip run smoothly, including getting about by public transport, weather tips, emergency phone numbers and useful websites.

Navigation In the Melbourne by Area chapter, we've given each area its own colour, which is also used on the locator maps throughout the book and the map on the inside front cover.

Maps The fold-out map accompanying this book is a comprehensive street plan of Melbourne. The grid on this fold-out map is the same as the grid on the locator maps within the book. We've given grid references within the book for each sight and listing.

Contents

Introducing Melbourne

Melbourne, the capital of the state of Victoria and the heart of the Pacific rim economy, is a lively, forward-looking city, with a modern skyline. Yet the city retains its prosperous Victorian past with its wide boulevards, fine public buildings and infrastructure.

Divided by the quiet waters of the Yarra River, Melbourne is the country's second-largest city after Sydney, with 3.8 million people representing over 70 cultures. From its Anglo-Saxon roots as the port for rich goldfields in the mid-19th century, Melbourne today exudes a multicultural air, influenced by the descendants of waves of post-World War II European migrants, especially those from Greece and Italy, and by the latter-day Asian arrivals, particularly the Vietnamese. This, combined with its long Chinese heritage and British origins, makes Melbourne one of Australia's most multicultural cities.

Living in the sporting and cultural events capital of Australia, Melburnians are as passionate about sport as they are about the arts. The unique Australian Rules Football code had its origins here and the city is home to Australia's best collection of art at the two National Gallery of Victoria locations.

For dining and shopping, there is no finer destination in Australia. With over 5,000 cafés and restaurants serving cuisines from far and wide, food lovers have a great choice, with alfresco dining all the rage. Many of the nation's best wines are produced in Victoria. You will find great shopping within the Central Business District (CBD) and nearby suburbs of Carlton, Fitzroy, South Yarra and Richmond—catering for all tastes and styles.

Only an hour's drive from the city you can see Australia's unique and often shy wildlife. The picturesque Dandenong Mountains on the city's edge are a favoured weekend destination, while the Mornington Peninsula is the perfect summer beach escape.

Facts + Figures

- **The most common language spoken after English is Mandarin (9.3 per cent)**
- **The oldest building is the Mitre Tavern: 1837**
- **Residents born overseas: 42.2 per cent**

MELBOURNE CUP

On the first Tuesday of November, Australia comes to a standstill, as people are glued to television sets to watch the nation's richest and most prestigious horse race, the Melbourne Cup. Run over 3,300m (2 miles), this handicap race carries prize money of 5 million Australian dollars. Everyone tries to pick the winner in this notoriously unpredictable race.

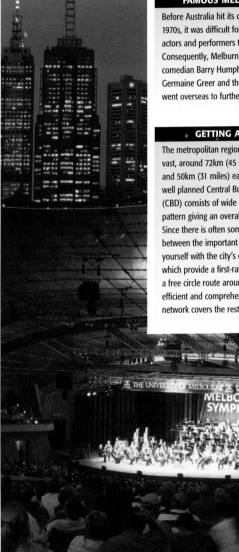

FAMOUS MELBURNIANS

Before Australia hit its cultural stride in the 1970s, it was difficult for talented writers, actors and performers to succeed here. Consequently, Melburnians such as comedian Barry Humphries, feminist writer Germaine Greer and the singer Nick Cave went overseas to further their careers.

GETTING AROUND

The metropolitan region of Melbourne is vast, around 72km (45 miles) north–south and 50km (31 miles) east–west. The city's well planned Central Business District (CBD) consists of wide streets in a grid pattern giving an overall sense of space. Since there is often some distance between the important sights, acquaint yourself with the city's excellent trams, which provide a first-rate service, including a free circle route around the CBD. An efficient and comprehensive rail and bus network covers the rest of the city.

A Short Stay in Melbourne

DAY 1

Morning Have an early breakfast and walk to the **Royal Botanic Gardens** (▷ 60–61) for a quiet stroll around the grounds. You might detour to the nearby Shrine of Remembrance, from where you have a fine vista back towards the city.

Mid-morning Hop on the St. Kilda Road tram that runs to the city and alight just over the Yarra River at Federation Square. Here you'll find the **Ian Potter Centre: NGV Australia** (▷ 44), and the Australian Centre for the Moving Image and nearby Birrarung Park. The city's main tourist information office is also here.

Lunch Head along Russell Street to **Chinatown** (▷ 24) for a slice of Asian culture—try one of the many dining options and a take look at the **Chinese Museum** (▷ 24).

Afternoon Continue on to Spring Street and the check out the old **Princess Theatre** (▷ 31) and the **State Parliament House** (▷ 31), the grandiose home to Australia's first government, before arriving at the classic old **Windsor Hotel** (▷ 31), where you can enjoy a sumptuous afternoon tea.

Dinner Hop on the City Circle Tram and alight at the Flinders Street station. Walk over the Princes Bridge to **Southbank** (▷ 62), where you'll find an array of dining options from a range of multicultural cuisines; some restaurants have river and city views.

Evening Just nearby, on St. Kilda Road, is **The Arts Centre** (▷ 56), where you can choose a cultural night out from a range of opera, musical and drama performances.

DAY 2

Morning Walk around the CBD and head for the **Laneways** (▷ 25). Be sure to try the chocolate samples at **Koko Black** (▷ 51) and have a coffee break.

Mid-morning Walk to the vibrant **Queen Victoria Market** (▷ 27), where you can look for bargain clothing and souvenirs. One section of the market is devoted to food, so you can buy some tasty treats for a picnic lunch.

Lunch Take the tram to **St. Kilda** (▷ 97) for a picnic lunch on the seashore. Walk along The Esplanade—there's an arts and crafts market here on Sundays (10am–5pm)—then head to nearby Acland Street's array of tempting pastry shops for a coffee break.

Afternoon Return via tram to the city and visit the **Melbourne Aquarium** (▷ 46), one of the most popular of the city's attractions, where you can see and touch a variety of marine creatures and dive with sharks. Take a tea break at the aquarium's Moorings Café.

Dinner The free City Circle Tram will take you to **NewQuay** (▷ 26) in the Docklands precinct, where you can choose from a wide range of waterside restaurants. There is an opportunity here to choose a restaurant with a great view of the harbour at the same time as being able to find a meal to suit your choice of cuisine.

Evening There are some great nightspots in the vicinity, including **James Squire Brewhouse** (▷ 36) if you like boutique beers. The new Waterfront City is the perfect place to relax and enjoy a drink after dinner by the harbour.

Top 25

▼ **The Arts Centre** ▷ 56
The centre of Melbourne's theatre, dance, opera and symphonic music.

Carlton ▷ 82 An art cinema, bookshop, dining and shopping precinct, with an Italian flavour.

Chinatown ▷ 24 The colourful and vibrant Asian core of the city, with Asian restaurants and food shops.

City Centre and Laneways ▷ 25 Melbourne's retail heart with stores, boutiques and dining surprises.

Docklands ▷ 26 The city's waterside growth area includes top restaurants, galleries and shops.

Eureka Skydeck 88 ▷ 57 Catch some amazing 360-degree views of the city and dare to enter The Edge.

Federation Square ▷ 42–43 The city's meeting place is an architectural icon and cultural draw.

Fitzroy ▷ 83 The city's most colourful suburb, where grunge rules—quirky bars and funky shops.

Fitzroy and Treasury Gardens ▷ 72–73 Floral beauty with Captain Cook's Cottage as a centrepiece.

Heide Museum of Modern Art ▷ 94 Celebrates the work of Australia's early Modernists.

Ian Potter Centre: NGV Australia ▷ 44 The nation's best collection of Australian art.

Immigration Museum ▷ 45 All about the city's immigrant communities.

Melbourne Aquarium ▷ 46–47 See-through tunnels reveal a display of sharks and rays.

Melbourne Cricket Ground ▷ 74 Australia's most famous sporting arena.

Melbourne Museum ▷ 84 Learn about the city's past and walk through a living indoor forest.

Melbourne Zoo ▷ 85 Home to the full range of Australia's fascinating wildlife, plus a world-class gorilla enclosure.

NGV International ▷ 58–59 Paintings, sculptures and decorative arts of the hghest order.

Old Melbourne Gaol ▷ 28–29 Grim, one-time home to notorious felons and the gallows.

Queen Victoria Market ▷ 27 Inexpensive clothing, souvenirs, and fresh produce are on offer here.

Rippon Lea and Como House ▷ 95 Take a look at how the wealthy lived in days gone by.

Royal Botanic Gardens ▷ 60–61 Stroll among one of the world's great plant collections, then relax on the lawns.

St. Kilda and Luna Park ▷ 97 Enjoy a trip to the seaside and its classic old fun park.

Scienceworks ▷ 96 Interactive displays to interest and entertain all ages, plus fantastic shows at the planetarium.

Southbank and the Crown Complex ▷ 62 Spend some leisure time by the banks of the Yarra River, shopping, dining and more.

The Yarra River ▷ 48–49 Seeing the city from the river gives a unique perspective.

These pages are a quick guide to the Top 25, which are described in more detail later. Here they are listed alphabetically, and the tinted background shows which area they are in.

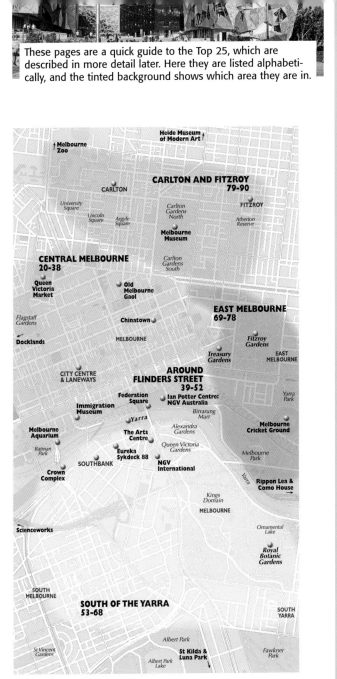

Heide Museum of Modern Art

Melbourne Zoo

CARLTON AND FITZROY 79-90

CARLTON

University Square

FITZROY

Lincoln Square

Argyle Square

Carlton Gardens North

Atherton Reserve

Melbourne Museum

CENTRAL MELBOURNE 20-38

Carlton Gardens South

Queen Victoria Market

Old Melbourne Gaol

Flagstaff Gardens

EAST MELBOURNE 69-78

Chinatown

Docklands

MELBOURNE

Fitzroy Gardens

Treasury Gardens

EAST MELBOURNE

CITY CENTRE & LANEWAYS

AROUND FLINDERS STREET 39-52

Federation Square

Ian Potter Centre: NGV Australia

Yarra Park

Immigration Museum

Birrarung Marr

Yarra

Melbourne Aquarium

The Arts Centre

Alexandra Gardens

Melbourne Cricket Ground

Batman Park

Eureka Sykdeck 88

Queen Victoria Gardens

Melbourne Park

SOUTHBANK

Crown Complex

NGV International

Rippon Lea & Como House

Kings Domain

MELBOURNE

Scienceworks

Ornamental Lake

Royal Botanic Gardens

SOUTH MELBOURNE

SOUTH OF THE YARRA 53-68

SOUTH YARRA

St Vincent Gardens

Albert Park

St Kilda & Luna Park

Fawkner Park

Albert Park Lake

Shopping

Melburnians love to shop and the great array of retail outlets, from upper end to budget, attests to this. In fact, the city really is the shopping capital of Australia.

Australiana

Original Australian design tends to be influenced by nature. Natural materials such as indigenous timbers are used to produce utilitarian bowls and decorative sculptures, regional clays are used in pottery, and wool is often crafted into what could best be described as 'wearable art'. When it comes to jewellery, Australian opals are much admired and reputable dealers seek to educate potential buyers by displaying rough stones and exhibits explaining how opals are mined. Lustrous South Sea pearls, in all sizes, are great buying, as are gemstones set in Australian gold, and the distinctive pink Argyle diamonds. Check out several shops before settling on a purchase.

Out and About

Melbourne's retail heart may be the streets and laneways of the CBD (▷ 25), but in a variety of nearby suburbs you'll find interesting specialty shops selling clothing, giftware, souvenirs, books, music and jewellery, plus any number of art galleries. Interesting retail arcades around the city include The Block Arcade, Australia on Collins, Collins Place, Melbourne Central, Melbourne's GPO and the Royal Arcade. Seek out the quirky little stores in the backstreets specialising in hand-made jewellery, one-off chic designs, chocolates and unusual gifts.

BARGAIN SHOPPING

The post-Christmas season, from late December into January, is bargain shopping time. So is mid-winter, in June and July. You can shop for clothing on a budget at any time in department and chain stores. Head to Richmond, where shops selling designer seconds and other well-priced clothes are plentiful. Inner-city suburbs offer bargains in second-hand clothing and many other items.

From cuddly toys to quirky clothes, Aboriginal objects to hand-made hats— shopping Melbourne style

International brand names are available from the big retail stores Myer and David Jones, as well as from shops at the upper end of Collins Street and in South Yarra and Toorak. Be sure to trawl colourful Brunswick Street in Fitzroy for grunge fashions and funky homeware, second-hand goods, books and alternative art.

Head for a Bargain

For discount retailing, start at the Queen Victoria Market, but check out DFO Spencer (▷ 35) in Spencer Street for several levels of designer clothing at factory outlet prices. Bridge Road and Swan Street in Richmond offer designer seconds and well-priced clothes are plentiful. Be sure to check out the Sunday arts and crafts markets at the Arts Centre and St. Kilda, and the Saturday book market at Federation Square. The Prahran Market (▷ 66) has fresh fruit and vegetables, and deli goods including organic produce. High Street in Armadale has over 1,000 antique dealers and 20 art galleries. If you have some extra time, make the trip to nearby attractive town of Daylesford, where Victoria's largest outdoor market is held at the old railway station.

Going Home

For that last-minute souvenir or gift, Melbourne Airport has a wide range of retail outlets selling food, fashion, souvenirs, plus the usual array of duty free-goods.

BOOKS ON AUSTRALIA

Photographic books documenting contemporary Melbourne make good souvenirs, and there are many. To find out what the city was like in the 19th century, read *The Rise and Fall of Marvellous Melbourne* by Graeme Davidson. To learn about the original inhabitants, read *Aboriginal Australians* by Richard Broome. Tim Flannery's *The Future Eaters* is a fascinating ecological history of Australia. For a really close look at the origins of Melbourne as the gateway to the Victorian goldfields, read Volume 3 of Manning Clark's *A History of Australia*.

Shopping by Theme

Whether you're looking for a department store, a quirky boutique, or something in between, you'll find it all in Melbourne. On this page shops are listed by theme. For a more detailed write-up, see the individual listings in Melbourne by Area.

AUSTRALIANA

Ken Duncan Gallery (▷ 65)
Kirra Australia Gallery (▷ 65)
Koorie Connections (▷ 35)
R M Williams (▷ 35)

BOOKS AND MUSIC

ABC Shop (▷ 34)
Angus & Robertson Bookworld (▷ 51)
Borders (▷ 65)
Brunswick Street Bookstore (▷ 88)
Collins Booksellers (▷ 34)
Hill of Content (▷ 35)
Kay Craddock (▷ 35)
Mary Martin Bookshop ▷ 65)
Middle Eight Music (▷ 66)
Mondo Music (▷ 88)
Music Swop Shop (▷ 88)
Readings (▷ 88)

FASHION

Alphaville (▷ 88)
Bobby's Cuts (▷ 51)
Country Road (▷ 34)
Dakota 501 (▷ 65)
Denim Deluxe (▷ 88)
Kundalini Rising (▷ 88)
Queen Clothing (▷ 66)
Saks (▷ 66)
Tomorrow Never Knows (▷ 88)

FOOD AND DRINK

A1 Middle East Food Store (▷ 103)

David Jones Food Hall (▷ 34)
De Bortoli Winery and Restaurant (▷ 103)
Flavours, Herbs & Spices (▷ 65)
Koko Black (▷ 51)
The Original Lolly Shop (▷ 88)
Phillippa's Bakery Provisions (▷ 103)
Richmond Hill Café and Larder (▷ 77)
Walter's Wine Bar (▷ 66)

JEWELLERY AND GEMS

Abbess Opal Mine (▷ 34)
Desert Gems (▷ 65)
Elizabeth's (▷ 65)
Kaiserman (▷ 65)
Makers Mark (▷ 35)
Rutherford Antiques (▷ 35)

MARKETS

Armadale Antique Centre (▷ 103)
Camberwell Sunday Market (▷ 103)
Greville Street Market (▷ 65)
Pipeworks Market (▷ 103)
Prahran Market (▷ 66)
Queen Victoria Market (▷ 27)
St. Kilda Esplanade Market (▷ 103)
South Melbourne (▷ 66)
The Sunday Art Market (▷ 66)

SHOPPING AREAS

Carlton (▷ 88)
Fitzroy (▷ 88)

Richmond (▷ 77)
St. Kilda (▷ 103)
Southgate (▷ 66)
South Yarra & Prahran (▷ 66)
Williamstown (▷ 103)

SHOPPING CENTRES

Australia on Collins (▷ 34)
The Block Arcade (▷ 34)
Brands United (▷ 77)
Collins Place (▷ 34)
Collins Street ('Paris End') (▷ 34)
David Jones (▷ 34)
DFO Spencer (▷ 35)
The Galleria (▷ 35)
Jam Factory (▷ 65)
Melbourne Central (▷ 35)
Myer (▷ 35)
Royal Arcade (▷ 35)

SPECIALIST SHOPS

Arts Centre Shop (▷ 65)
Australian Geographic Shop (▷ 34)
Circa Vintage Clothing (▷ 88)
City Hatters (▷ 51)
Emil's Shoe Repair (▷ 65)
En Route (▷ 65)
Ishka Handcrafts (▷ 88)
Make Designed Objects (▷ 88)
Matchbox (▷ 103)
Melbourne Surf Shop (▷ 35)
National Wool Museum Shop (▷ 103)
Savill Galleries (▷ 66)
The Workshop (▷ 66)

Melbourne by Night

Melbourne's diverse nightlife options include something for everyone—from the high arts of opera, classical music and cutting-edge drama to a night on the town at a nightclub or pub.

Cultural Melbourne

The Arts Centre (▷ 56) presents excellent opera, ballet and classical music performances. The orchestra performs at the Hamer Hall, the State Theatre hosts opera, and the centre's Playhouse presents a variety of theatrical productions. Classical music concerts are also given at the Melbourne Town Hall, the Conservatorium of Music and the Sidney Myer Music Bowl. Lavish musicals can be enjoyed in Melbourne's fabulous old theatres, such as The Princess and Her Majesty's, while the Last Laugh Comedy Club (▷ 36) has a dinner show with professional stand-up acts on Friday and Saturday nights.

Out on the Town

For that special night out you will find national and international stars performing at the Crown Entertainment Complex (▷ 62), which includes the huge Crown Casino with the usual blackjack, roulette, craps and myriad slot machines. The complex also has 17 bars, 85 restaurants and several nightclubs. Melbourne has a vibrant gay and lesbian scene, especially in the area around Commercial Road in South Yarra. Every Friday, *The Age* newspaper publishes *EG*, an entertainment guide that lists the various options around the city and suburbs. City Search (www.melbourne.citysearch.com.au) is another good source of information.

GETTING HOME LATE AT NIGHT

There are special public transport arrangements in place for Friday and Saturday nights. While trams stop running at 11pm from Sunday to Thursday, this is extended to 1am on Friday and Saturday nights. The Nightrider bus service operates between 12.30am and 4.30am on Saturday and Sunday mornings and suburban trains run to 1am.

Dazzling scenes of Melbourne illuminated at night

Eating Out

People from more than 140 nations make Melbourne their home, so there may be some truth in the maxim that you can eat your way around the world here. The city has more than 5,000 restaurants, most offering a range of Victoria's fine wines.

Home Talent
Australian chefs have made a name for them-selves worldwide and Modern Australian dishes, which fuse European and Asian food styles with local ingredients, has arrived as a distinct cutting-edge cuisine. Dishes incorporating Aboriginal foods containing bush tucker ingredi-ents, such as kangaroo, emu, crocodile and native fruits and nuts, have their own unique flavour. Greek restaurants are everywhere, and, not surprisingly, seafood is popular in this bayside city. Local specialties include Melbourne rock oysters, kingfish, huge prawns, Tasmanian scallops and South Australian tuna. Appropriately, many seafood restaurants have waterfront locations, where you can buy excellent fish and chips to take away—St. Kilda, NewQuay and Williamstown are great spots for alfresco dining.

Melbourne's Asian Restaurants
The city's best Chinese cuisine is at the pinna-cle of quality, along with refined cuisine from Indonesia, Burma, Taiwan, Korea, Laos and other Asian countries. Most Asian restaurants are reasonably priced and many are BYO—bring your own alcohol. The best Thai restaurants are equal to those found anywhere outside Thailand. Thai dishes are light and tasty—made with fresh produce and delicate spices and herbs. Vietnam-ese cuisine rivals Thai cuisine in popularity.

HOME GROWN
Victoria has a strong rural industry supplying prime beef and lamb, all types of seafood, and fresh fruit and vegetables. And dairy produce, in the form of specialty cheeses and yoghurts is particularly worth seeking out. Restaurants draw on this produce for their ingredients.

Dining alfresco is a popular pastime for Melburnians and visitors alike

Restaurants by Cuisine

There are restaurants to suit all tastes and budgets in Melbourne. On this page they are listed by cuisine. For a more detailed description of each restaurant, see Melbourne by Area.

CAFÉS

Arriverderci Aroma (▷ 37)
Blue Train Café (▷ 52)
Café Chinotto (▷ 52)
The Commune (▷ 78)
The Deck (▷ 68)
George Street Café (▷ 78)
The Pavilion (▷ 78)
Pellegrini's Espresso Bar (▷ 38)
Rathdowne Street Food Store (▷ 90)
Retro Café (▷ 90)

CONTEMPORARY

Arintji (▷ 52)
Becco (▷ 37)
Blakes (▷ 52)
Circa (▷ 106)
Donovans (▷ 106)
Fenix (▷ 78)
Fifteen (▷ 38)
The Groove Train (▷ 68)
Hairy Canary (▷ 38)
Jimmy Watson's Wine Bar & Restaurant (▷ 90)
Mecca (▷ 52)
The Point (▷ 68)

Richmond Hill Café & Larder (▷ 78)
Sapore (▷ 106)

EUROPEAN

Bar Lourinha (▷ 37)
Café Dionysos (▷ 90)
Caffè e Cucina (▷ 68)
City Wine Shop (▷ 37)
European (▷ 37)
France Soir (▷ 68)
Grossi Florentino (▷ 38)
Hofbrauhaus (▷ 38)
Pireaus Blues (▷ 90)
Radii (▷ 78)
Scusa Mi (▷ 68)
Tsindos (▷ 38)
Zampelis Café Greco (▷ 68)

MISCELLANEOUS ASIAN

Bokchoy Tang (▷ 52)
Burmese House (▷ 78)
Chine on Paramount (▷ 37)
Flower Drum (▷ 38)
Kenzan (▷ 52)
Kuni's (▷ 38)
Mask of China (▷ 38)
Near East (▷ 68)

Penang Affair (▷ 90)
Warung Agus (▷ 38)

OUT OF TOWN

The Healesville Hotel (▷ 106)
Kenlock Licensed Restaurant (▷ 106)
Ozone Hotel (▷ 106)
Peppers Delgany (▷ 106)
Wild Oak Café (▷ 106)
Yarra Valley Dairy (▷ 106)

SEAFOOD

Harry's (▷ 106)
Melbourne Oyster Bar (▷ 38)
Sails on the Bay (▷ 106)
Toofeys (▷ 90)

THAI/VIETNAMESE

The Gate (▷ 78)
Lemongrass (▷ 90)
Min Tan II (▷ 78)
Sukhothai (▷ 90)
Sweet Basil (▷ 68)
Thai Thani (▷ 90)
Viet's Quan (▷ 68)

If You Like...

However you'd like to spend your time in Melbourne, these top suggestions should help you tailor your ideal visit. Each sight or listing has a fuller write-up in Melbourne by Area.

SAMPLING LOCAL CUISINE

Dishes with a hint of Italy are prepared using only the best of local seasonal produce at Fifteen (▷ 38).

Melbourne's finest Cantonese cuisine can be sampled at the elegant Flower Drum (▷ 38) in Chinatown.

OUTDOOR DINING

Fancy breakfast outside—then try The Pavilion (▷ 78) in Fitzroy Gardens with its tasty café-style fare.

The free City Circle Tram will take you to New-Quay (▷ 26) in the Docklands precinct, where you can choose from a range of waterside restaurants.

Pasta and black truffle sauce (top); flowers in Fitzroy Gardens (above)

BRAND-NAME CLOTHES

Brands United (▷ 77) sells quality brand clothing as well as men's and women's underwear and lingerie.

Australia on Collins (▷ 34), in the city centre, houses a number of specialty shops featuring international brand names.

FREE THINGS

At the Royal Botanic Gardens (▷ 60–61) you can stroll among one of the world's great plant collections.

See some of the world's most admired paintings, sculptures and decorative arts at the NGV International (▷ 58–59).

Quality clothing for sale (above right); plenty of space for displaying the NGV International's superb international art collection (right)

local culture meets modern lifestyle (below)

LEARNING ABOUT LOCAL CULTURE

The nation's best collection of Australian art with many Impressionist icons, can be found in the Ian Potter Centre (▷ 44) at Federation Square.
Koorie Connections (▷ 35) features works by contemporary Aboriginal artists, plus crafts, including the ubiquitous boomerang.

GOING OUT ON THE TOWN

Dress in ski gear and make your way to Chill On Ice Bar (▷ 36), where the cocktails are served from a bar made of ice.
James Squire Brewhouse (▷ 36) serves James Squire beers and also offers an extensive range of cocktails.

STAYING AT BUDGET HOTELS

At the City Centre Budget Hotel (▷ 109), your accommodation is less than A$100 a night and you get wireless internet.
Near the Queen Victoria Market is Global Backpackers (▷ 109) where you'll find good basic accommodation and an indoor climbing wall.

Backpackers on a budget (above)

ENTERTAINING THE KIDS

Scienceworks (▷ 96) is fun for kids and adults, with lots of hand-on exhibits. Don't miss the Lightning Room.
The Eastern Hill Fire Museum (▷ 75) has a display of fire-fighting memorabilia and Australia's largest collection of restored fire trucks.

The Planetarium at the Scienceworks museum (left)

A GIRLS' NIGHT OUT

Try one of Melbourne's favourite new pubs,
The Transport Hotel (▷ 51) at Federation
Square, with live music and DJ's every
night of the week.

Also known as Africa Bar, check out
Planet Afrik (▷ 89) in Carlton, to sip safari
cocktails and enjoy fantastic, mesmorising
West African music.

*Melbourne leisure—out
on the town or out in
the woods (below)*

A WALK ON THE WILD SIDE

Phillip Island (▷ 101) has a
substantial waterbird population
and there are elevated boardwalks
through bushland for easy viewing. Be sure not to miss the
penguins.

**The scenic Dandenong
Ranges** (▷ 99) are less than an hour's
drive from the CBD, and have lots of mountain
forest walking trails.

CUTTING-EDGE ARCHITECTURE

Going green—The 10-storey office building, CH_2
(▷ 30), incorporates all aspects of sustainability in
its all-embracing eco design.

The Eureka Skydeck 88 (▷ 57) is the observation deck at the top of the Eureka Tower and offers
panoramic viewing of Melbourne and surrounds.

*The striking Eureka
Tower (above)*

BIRDS AND ANIMALS

One of Australia's top wildlife parks is
Healesville Sanctuary (▷ 99), set in the
foothills of the scenic Yarra Valley.

Home to the full range of Australia's
wildlife, Melbourne Zoo (▷ 85) also
has a world-class gorilla enclosure, set in
a rainforest.

*A lowland gorilla having fun at the excellent
Melbourne Zoo (right)*

Melbourne by Area

Central Melbourne, the shopping and dining epicentre of the city, has been revitalized by an influx of residents and waterside development in the new Docklands district.

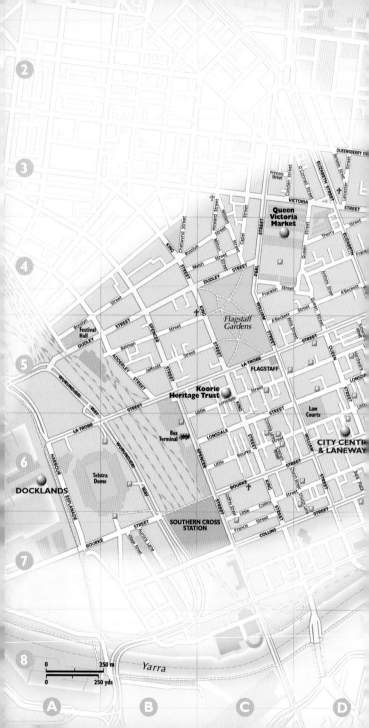

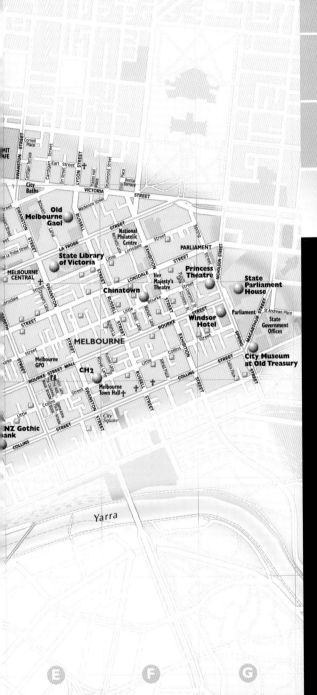

SMIT
AFE

Cornell
Place

SWANSTON

STREET

Cardigan Terrace

Cardigan Street

Earl

Orr Street

Street

LYGON

Palmerston Place

Drummond Place

STREET

Rental
Terrace

Street

City
Baths

Bowen

Street

Street

VICTORIA

STREET

Old
Melbourne
Gaol

Mackenzie street

Street

RUSSELL

STREET

SWANSTON

STREET

Bouverie

Street

La Trobe Place

LA TROBE

STREET

State Library
of Victoria

National
Philatelic
Centre

Little

EXHIBITION

Lonsdale

street

Street

PARLIAMENT

STREET

MELBOURNE
CENTRAL

Lonsdale

Street

STREET

LONSDALE

SWANSTON

STREET

RUSSELL

STREET

Chinatown

Her
Majesty's
Theatre

Bourke

Street

Little Lonsdale

STREET

Princess
Theatre

NICHOLSON STREET

SPRING

State
Parliament
House

STREET

Street

Corrs Lane

Windsor
Hotel

Parliament

MACARTHUR STREET

St Andrews Place

State
Government
Offices

AMEL

STREET

urke

Street

MELBOURNE

BOURKE

STREET

Little

Corporation Lane

RUSSELL

Little

Collins

Street

EXHIBITION

STREET

STREET

STREET

SWANSTON

Royal Lane

Russell Lane

Little

City Museum
at Old Treasury

Melbourne
GPO

BOURKE STREET MALL

CH2

Melbourne
Town Hall

Collins

Street

Russell

Alfred Place

Place

SPRING

Collins

Street

STREET

STREET

NZ Gothic
Bank

COLLINS

Little

Collins

Street

SWANSTON

STREET

STREET

City
Square

STREET

RUSSELL

Yarra

E   F   G

Chinatown

The streets behind the stone lions, where the city's Chinatown comes alive on carnival day

The Chinese community has been settled in bustling Little Bourke Street since the gold-rush days of the 1850s. Today, excellent restaurants and specialist shops sit next to herbalists and small shops selling Chinese goods and food.

The backstreets Chinese gates and two stone lions mark this distinctive part of Little Bourke Street, between Exhibition and Swanston streets, although it spills over into the adjoining streets and lanes. After the gold rush, many Chinese immigrants opened shops, furniture factories and other businesses here, and some of the 19th-century Victorian buildings commissioned by Chinese businessmen and designed by notable architects of the day still stand. Today, Asian supermarkets, restaurants and cake shops cater for Chinese tastes.

Chinese Museum In this museum in Cohen Place, off Little Bourke Street, there are excellent photographic exhibits on the history and culture of the Chinese people in Australia, together with an interesting walk-through re-creation of the experience of the Chinese on the goldfields in early Victoria. Among the exhibits is a life-size replica of a Warrior General from the second century BC, the only such replica outside China, and Dai Loong, reputedly the world's longest processional dragon that is paraded by 100 men through the streets each year at the Moomba Festival in March, a 10-day carnival with cultural and sporting events.

Just relaxing or taking a boat down the river, there's plenty do in central Melbourne

City Centre and Laneways

Compact and easy to explore, the centre of Melbourne is set out in a rectangular grid. When you get tired of walking, just jump on a tram—the one that operates around the perimeter of the CBD is free.

City centre Focusing on the Central Business District or CBD, you will find most of the main department stores, hotels, offices and banks, as well as the fine old Victorian churches, theatres and public institutions that give Melbourne its personality in this central area. Excellent restaurants and cafés are scattered throughout the city centre. Within walking distance, across the Yarra River to the south, are parks and gardens, The Arts Centre and National Gallery of Victoria, the Southgate shopping and dining complex on Southbank, and Crown Casino. The best way to get a sense of the place is on foot, with occasional rides on the free City Circle Tram.

Melbourne's meeting place On the edge of the CBD, Federation Square (▷ 42–43) is the size of a city block. The excellent visitor centre here will provide comprehensive help with your travel plans.

Shopping Melbourne has great shopping opportunities. The retail area is bounded roughly by Elizabeth, Collins, Spring and La Trobe streets. Check out the city's lanes and arcades, especially the Royal and Block Arcades. Look for Hardware Lane, a stretch of old warehouses between Bourke and Lonsdale streets, converted into restaurants, bars and shops.

THE BASICS

✚ D6
✉ Melbourne Visitor Information Centre, Federation Square, corner of Swanston and Flinders streets
☎ 9658 9658
🕐 Daily 9–6
🍴 Many cafés, restaurants and shops
🚃 City Circle Tram
♿ Varies
❓ Shopping hours may vary, but city shops are generally open Mon–Thu 10–6, Fri 10–9, Sat–Sun 10–5.
Be sure to book a Hidden Secrets Tour: www.hiddensecretstour.com
☎ 9329 9665

HIGHLIGHTS

● Federation Square
● Lanes and arcades
● Specialist shops
● Historic buildings

Docklands

The NewQuay area of Melbourne's Docklands has some striking modern sculpture

Just minutes away from Melbourne's CBD, Docklands is the city's latest waterfront development, with a dynamic mix of restaurants, galleries, shops and leisure activities, set alongside the Yarra River and Victoria Harbour.

Ongoing development About the same size as the Melbourne CBD, Docklands will be developed in stages over the next 15 years. Marinas, promenades, parklands, fine restaurants and residential areas are already in place and are connected to the city by excellent public transport, scenic walkways and cycling lanes.

What's going on? NewQuay, at the northwestern edge of the harbour, has many restaurants offering a wide range of cuisines, cafes, bars and fashionable shops—all situated along the promenade, with stunning harbour and city views. Waterfront City is a vibrant mix of dining, entertainment, retail, residential and commercial elements. Many seasonal events take place in the public Piazza, which can hold up to 10,000 people. The Southern Star Observation Wheel is due to be completed by late 2008. The Wheel will be as tall as a 38-storey building, and its 21 air-conditioned pods will each carry 20 people. The half-hour ride will give you spectacular views.

Over the water Webb Bridge provides a pedestrian and cycle crossing to residential Yarra's Edge. Here you'll find excellent restaurants and a place for a quiet stroll along the riverfront promenade.

Queen Victoria Market

The array of mouth-watering produce on sale at the bustling Queen Victoria Market

Some of the original buildings still stand at Australia's biggest and most popular outdoor market, which offers just about everything from food, footwear and clothing to plants, art and souvenirs.

History Just a few minutes' walk from the city centre, this bustling, chaotic retail complex is the city's largest market, with over a thousand stalls on 7ha (17 acres). The complex is the last of several city markets. Many of the present buildings date back to the 19th century, including the Meat Hall (1869), Sheds A to F (1878) and the two-storey shops on Victoria Street (1887).

Markets The colourful traders are an attraction in their own right, promoting their wares and bantering with passers-by. In the Lower Market are the Meat Hall, with meat, fish and game; the Dairy Hall, featuring delicatessens and bakeries; and a section with fresh fruit and vegetables, as well as a huge range of ready-to-eat foods. On a nearby rise, a stretch of open-sided sheds, known as the Upper Market, houses an enormous variety of fresh produce, clothing and souvenirs. From Friday to Sunday, a wine market operates.

Guided tours The Foodies Dream Tour provides a chance to taste Australian cheeses, nuts, preserves, meats and exotic tropical fruits, while the Heritage Market Tour takes you through the market's original buildings and describes a century of its fascinating past. Note that the Heritage Tour is for groups only.

THE BASICS

➕ C4
✉ Corner of Elizabeth and Victoria streets
☎ Information: 9320 5822. Tours: 9320 5835
🕐 Tue, Thu 6–2, Fri 6–6, Sat 6–3, Sun 9–4
🍴 Many cafés and restaurants nearby and plenty of stalls selling snack food and coffee
Ⓜ Melbourne Central
🚃 Any tram in Elizabeth northbound to stop 12
♿ Moderate

HIGHLIGHTS

● The stallholders
● Stalls selling exotic tropical fruits and Australian cheeses
● Historic buildings
● Market tours
● Weekend Wine Market

Old Melbourne Gaol

TOP 25

Ned Kelly's death mask (middle) on display at the notorious Old Melbourne Gaol

THE BASICS

www.oldmelbournegaol.com.au

✚ E4

✉ Russell Street

☎ 9663 7228

⏰ Daily 9.30–5

🚃 City Circle Tram

♿ Limited

💷 Moderate

❓ Tour groups by arrangement. 'Such a Life', a fascinating look at Ned Kelly's life and legend, is performed every Sat at 12.30 and 2

HIGHLIGHTS

● Bluestone building
● Death masks
● Ned Kelly memorabilia
● Candlelight Night Tours
● Prisoners' Stories

This historic bluestone prison is fixed in national folklore as the place where Australia's most famous bushranger, Ned Kelly, was hanged. Here you can see the gallows and the death masks of several unfortunates.

A gruesome past This grim, gloomy place, with thick walls, small cells and heavy iron doors, is Victoria's oldest surviving penal establishment. To spend some time within its walls is to begin to understand the realities of prison life in the 19th century. Begun in 1841 and completed in 1864, it was designed along the lines of the Pentonville Modern Prison in London and consists of three levels of cells. The gallows, where 135 men and women were hanged, is the centrepiece of the complex. The death masks of some of those executed are on display, along with their stories. The most famous hanging was that of the bushranger Ned Kelly, one of the nation's folk heroes, an outlaw executed in 1889, whose famous last words were, 'Such is life'. A wooden tableau depicts the Kelly execution and nightly performances re-create the prison's gruesome past. The present cell block was in use until 1929 when the last prisoners were transferred to other prisons.

In the cells The penal museum presents displays and provides information on many infamous inmates, displays the Hangman's Box with its original contents and chronicles incarcerations. The flogging frame is on view along with the punishment instruments.

More to See

ANZ GOTHIC BANK
This highly decorated Gothic revival bank, completed in 1887, has been compared to the Doge's Palace in Venice. Its magnificent interior, with gold leaf ornamentation amid graceful arches and pillars, features decorative shields from the countries and cities around the world that the original bank, the England, Scottish and Australian Bank, traded with.
✚ D6 ✉ 386 Collins Street ☎ 9273 5555 ⊙ Mon–Fri 9.30–4 🚋 City Circle Tram ♿ Free

CH_2
This visionary new 'green' 10-storey office building has sustainability features incorporated into every conceivable aspect of its design. Tour this remarkable building to see its light- harvesting devices, solar hot water collectors, photovoltaic cells, co-generation plant, multi-use water treatment plant, vertical landscaping and much more.
✚ E5 ✉ 240 Little Collins Street ☎ 9658 9658 ⊙ Tue–Thu: meet in the lobby at 1.50 🚋 City Circle Tram ♿ Free

CITY MUSEUM AT OLD TREASURY
This superb example of neoclassical architecture, one the city's finest buildings, was built between 1858 and 1862 as the repository for the young colony's gold reserves. Now a museum, it showcases the wealth of the goldrush era and presents diverse exhibitions highlighting the city's history. It is next door to the pleasant Treasury Gardens.
✚ G5 ✉ Spring Street ☎ 9651 2233 ⊙ Mon–Fri 9–4.30, Sat–Sun 10–4 🚋 City Circle Tram ♿ Moderate

KOORIE HERITAGE TRUST
The trust's Cultural Centre has two gallery spaces featuring works by contemporary Aboriginal artists, plus a permanent exhibition that includes traditional artefacts and rare books. Its oral history unit provides a fascinating insight into the rich history and culture of Australia's southeastern indigenous people.
✚ C5 ✉ King Street, corner Little Lonsdale Street ☎ 9602 4333 ⊙ Daily 10–4

Fusion architecture—the new towers over the old

The City Museum

🚊 City Circle Tram to La Trobe and King streets 🎟 Free

PRINCESS THEATRE
One of the world's grand old theatres, this study in Victorian splendour was built as a palace for the arts in 1854, a time when live theatre was the greatest of attractions. Today it mounts major musical productions.
➕ G5 ✉ 163 Spring Street ☎ 9663 3300 🕐 Daily 🍴 Café 🚊 City Circle Tram 🎟 Free

STATE LIBRARY OF VICTORIA
This large library complex, with an impressive domed reading room, is an attraction in its own right. There are changing exhibitions and a vast collection of books that can be browsed through on request.
➕ E4 ✉ 328 Swanston Street ☎ 8664 7002 🕐 Mon–Thu 10–9, Fri–Sun 10–6. Closed public hols 🚊 City Circle Tram 🎟 Free

STATE PARLIAMENT HOUSE
Built during the gold rush in 1856, and amended with a wide flight of bluestone steps and towering Doric columns in 1892, this grand building was the first home of the Australian Parliament, until it moved to Canberra in 1927. You can attend a session when the State Parliament is sitting, and there are daily tours (▷ 32).
➕ G5 ✉ Spring Street ☎ 9651 8568 🕐 Tours: Mon–Fri 10–3 🚊 City Circle Tram 🎟 Free

WINDSOR HOTEL
A Melbourne landmark listed by the National Trust and the grandest hotel in Australia, the meticulously restored Windsor has all the elegance of a luxury 19th-century hotel. Even if you don't stay here, be sure to pop in to admire the sweeping, wrought-iron staircase, the ornately detailed foyer and the rich detail of the Grand Ballroom. The hotel is in Spring Street, just opposite the State Parliament House.
➕ G5 ✉ 111 Spring Street ☎ 9633 6000 🕐 24-hour reception 🚊 City Circle Tram 🎟 Free for a look

A good meeting place—the entrance to the State Parliament House

City Heritage Walk

Learn about Melbourne's fascinating past on this walk through the city's heritage precincts, streets, arcades and laneways.

DISTANCE: 4km (2.5 miles)   **ALLOW:** 3 hours

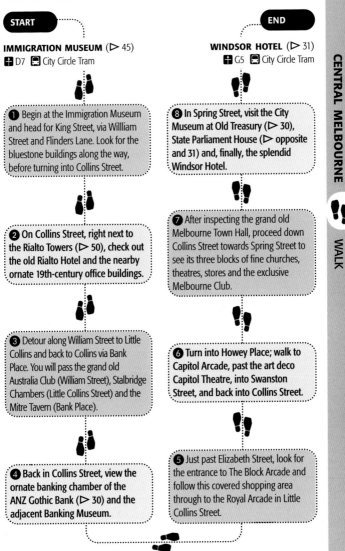

START

IMMIGRATION MUSEUM (▷ 45)
➕ D7 🚌 City Circle Tram

1 Begin at the Immigration Museum and head for King Street, via William Street and Flinders Lane. Look for the bluestone buildings along the way, before turning into Collins Street.

2 On Collins Street, right next to the Rialto Towers (▷ 50), check out the old Rialto Hotel and the nearby ornate 19th-century office buildings.

3 Detour along William Street to Little Collins and back to Collins via Bank Place. You will pass the grand old Australia Club (William Street), Stalbridge Chambers (Little Collins Street) and the Mitre Tavern (Bank Place).

4 Back in Collins Street, view the ornate banking chamber of the ANZ Gothic Bank (▷ 30) and the adjacent Banking Museum.

END

WINDSOR HOTEL (▷ 31)
➕ G5 🚌 City Circle Tram

8 In Spring Street, visit the City Museum at Old Treasury (▷ 30), State Parliament House (▷ opposite and 31) and, finally, the splendid Windsor Hotel.

7 After inspecting the grand old Melbourne Town Hall, proceed down Collins Street towards Spring Street to see its three blocks of fine churches, theatres, stores and the exclusive Melbourne Club.

6 Turn into Howey Place; walk to Capitol Arcade, past the art deco Capitol Theatre, into Swanston Street, and back into Collins Street.

5 Just past Elizabeth Street, look for the entrance to The Block Arcade and follow this covered shopping area through to the Royal Arcade in Little Collins Street.

Shopping

ABBESS OPAL MINE
Good opal stones and jewellery, as well as coin watches, Australian pearls, woollens and kangaroo and sheepskin products.
➕ E5 ✉ 218–220 Swanston Street ☎ 9639 2188 🚋 City Circle Tram

ABC SHOP
Operated by the Australian Broadcasting Corporation, this interesting shop offers books, videos, music and audio cassettes, CDs, toys and clothes relating to Australian TV and radio programmes.
➕ E6 ✉ Corner of Elizabeth and Little Bourke streets ☎ 9626 1167 🚋 City Circle Tram

AUSTRALIAN GEOGRAPHIC SHOP
Australia's best artists, writers, photographers, craftspeople and designers join forces to produce clothing, prints, stationery, bird houses, telescopes and more.
➕ E5 ✉ Level 1, Melbourne Central ☎ 9639 2478 🚋 City Circle Tram

AUSTRALIA ON COLLINS
Over 65 specialist shops under one roof provide the best in fashion, food and housewares.
➕ E6 ✉ 260 Collins Street ☎ 9650 4355 🚋 City Circle Tram

THE BLOCK ARCADE
Opened in 1892, this National Trust-classified arcade has an intricately tiled floor, decorative ironwork, stained-glass windows and over 30 shops on three levels.
➕ E6 ✉ 282 Collins Street ☎ 9654 5244 🚋 City Circle Tram

COLLINS BOOKSELLERS
New books plus a good general backlist selection, and many discounted recent titles.
➕ F6 ✉ 104 Elizabeth Street ☎ 9650 9755 🚋 City Circle Tram

COLLINS PLACE
This large, stylish and popular shopping centre, in the heart of Collins Street, has many specialist shops.
➕ G5 ✉ Collins Street ☎ 9655 3600 🚋 City Circle Tram

COLLINS STREET ('PARIS END')
Many exclusive boutiques selling brand names are along this elegant stretch of Collins Street, between Swanston and Spring streets.
➕ G5 ✉ Collins Street 🚋 City Circle Tram

COUNTRY ROAD
An Australian success story, with shops abroad as well as in Melbourne Central, Carlton, South Yarra and Brighton, Country Road specializes in casual clothes for men and women, and home furnishings.
➕ E5 ✉ Melbourne Central ☎ 9663 1766 🚋 City Circle Tram

DAVID JONES
Known to the locals as DJs, this alternative to Myer sells quality goods. Excellent food hall in the Bourke Street shop.
➕ D6 ✉ Little Bourke, Bourke and Little Collins streets ☎ 9643 2222 🚋 City Circle Tram

DAVID JONES FOOD HALL
The lower level of this food hall is one of the city's most exclusive food shops. The great variety of produce includes

---

AUSTRALIAN DELICACIES
To get an idea of the best Australian produce, be sure to visit the Queen Victoria Market (▷ 27), where stall holders allow you to sample cheeses, meats and exotic fruits. Look for cheese from the Yarra Valley and Tasmania, and seafood from the cooler southern oceans--everything from scallops to Tasmanian smoked salmon (specialist fishmongers will cook your selection). Fruits grown in Victoria include strawberries, pears and apples. Vegetables such as snow peas, asparagus and broccoli are plentiful, as well as the only native nut to hit the world stage, the macadamia.

Australian wines, beers, cheeses, meats, seafood, fruit and vegetables.
🏢 D6 ✉ 299 Bourke Street ☎ 9643 2222 🚋 City Circle Tram

DFO SPENCER
Over 100 big-name brands under one roof, with discounts of up to 70 per cent off fashion and accessories.
🏢 C6 ✉ 1/201 Spencer Street ☎ 8689 7555 🚉 Southern Cross

THE GALLERIA
Interesting collection of fashion and gift shops.
🏢 E6 ✉ Corner of Elizabeth and Bourke streets ☎ 9675 6416 🚋 City Circle Tram

HILL OF CONTENT
A bookshop that is solid in current titles, with some specials and an excellent selection of cookbooks.
🏢 F5 ✉ 86 Bourke Street ☎ 9662 9472 🚋 City Circle Tram

KAY CRADDOCK
One of Melbourne's top secondhand and rare books dealers.
🏢 E6 ✉ 156 Collins Street ☎ 9654 8506 🕐 Mon–Sat 9–5 🚋 City Circle Tram

KOORIE CONNECTIONS
Authentic Aboriginal arts and crafts gallery owned and operated by Aboriginal people.
🏢 D3 ✉ 155 Victoria Street ☎ 9326 9824 🚋 City Circle Tram

MAKERS MARK
Representing Australia's finest studio jewellers and craftspeople, with designs made from South Sea pearls and Argyle diamonds.
🏢 G6 ✉ 88 Collins Street ☎ 9650 3444 🚋 City Circle Tram

MELBOURNE CENTRAL
This centre, covering two city blocks, houses over 160 specialist shops. There are also cafés, restaurants and an original building, once used in the manufacture of gunshot.
🏢 E4 ✉ Corner of Swanston and La Trobe streets ☎ 9922 1100 🚋 City Circle Tram

MELBOURNE SURF SHOP
Everything for the surfer, from boards to beachwear, including the popular

SHOPPING TOURS
To explore out-of-the-way bargain shopping districts, you might want to call one of the following operators, which organize guided shopping tours. Shopping Spree Tours (☎ 9596 6600) specializes in warehouse shopping for clothing and other goods at wholesale prices, and personalized packages and upmarket tours. The Melbourne Ambassadors Specialist Shopping Tour (☎ 99639 4044) is personalized, but pricey.

Billabong, Rip Curl and Hot Tuna brands.
🏢 E6 ✉ Tivoli Arcade, 251 Bourke Street ☎ 9654 8403 🚋 City Circle Tram

MYER
The biggest department store in the southern hemisphere sells a wide range of fashion, designer housewares, gifts and cosmetics.
🏢 D6 ✉ Lonsdale, Little Bourke and Bourke streets ☎ 9661 1111 🚋 City Circle Tram

QUEEN VICTORIA MARKET
See page 27.

R M WILLIAMS
Authentic Australian outback clothing and traditional Aussie footwear.
🏢 E6 ✉ Melbourne Central, 300 Lonsdale Street ☎ 9663 7126 🚋 City Circle Tram

ROYAL ARCADE
Australia's oldest retail arcade, the 'Royal' contains 30 shops that sell fashion and gifts, all overseen by two statues of Gog and Magog, giants from British folklore.
🏢 E6 ✉ 308 Little Collins Street 🚋 City Circle Tram

RUTHERFORD ANTIQUES
Purveys a superb range of fine sterling silver and antique jewellery, from Georgian to art deco.
🏢 E6 ✉ 182 Collins Street ☎ 9650 7878 🚋 City Circle Tram

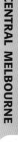

Entertainment and Nightlife

BAR CODE

This unique entertainment venue has a fully licensed bar plus the latest high tech interactive video games, a live DJ booth, neon-lit pool tables and contemporary lounge area.

➕ E4 ✉ 211 La Trobe Street, Melbourne Central (level 3) ☎ 9694 1230 🕐 Daily 10am–3am 🚋 City Circle Tram

BENNETTS LANE JAZZ CLUB

One of the best in Melbourne, this small jazz venue attracts top names playing a variety of jazz styles.

➕ F4 ✉ 25 Bennetts Lane ☎ 9663 2856 🕐 Nightly 🚋 City Circle Tram

CHILL ON ICE BAR

Billed as 'Seriously frigid fun!' Here you'll be dressed in ski gear and ugg boots, before you make your way to the ice lounge, where specially created ice-based cocktails are served from a bar made of ice.

➕ E4 ✉ 296 Russell Street ☎ 9663 3877 🕐 Mon–Thu noon–late, Fri noon–1am 🚋 City Circle Tram

CITY BATHS

This historic swimming complex is the place to get in a few laps or to just cool off on a hot day. Also has a gym, Jacuzzis, saunas and squash courts.

➕ E4 ✉ 420 Swanston Street ☎ 9663 5888

🕐 Mon–Fri 6am–10pm, Sat–Sun 8–6 🚋 Swanston Street Tram

COMEDY THEATRE

This delightful small theatre, modelled on a Florentine palace, with a Spanish-style interior, hosts a variety of shows.

➕ F5 ✉ 240 Exhibition Street ☎ 9299 9800 🚋 City Circle Tram

COOKIE

High ceilings, bluestone stairway, balconies overlooking Swanston Street and an incredibly long bar are features of this friendly, spacious establishment.

➕ E5 ✉ 252 Swanston Street Street ☎ 9663 7660 🕐 noon–3am 🚋 City Circle Tram

GIN PALACE

Where serious drinkers

BUYING A TICKET

There are several ways of obtaining tickets for theatre, live music concerts and other events. You can visit the box offices, or purchase by credit card from ticketing agencies such as Ticketmaster (☎ 136 166) and Ticketek (☎ 132 849). At Half Tix (☎ 1900 939 436), a booth in Bourke Street Mall, you can get discounted tickets on the day of performance. At the latter, tickets must be bought in person and you must pay in cash (Mon 10–2, Tue–Fri 11–6, Sat 10–2).

come for the classic martinis and the stylish ambience.

➕ E6 ✉ 190 Little Collins Street (enter from Russell Place) ☎ 9654 0533 🕐 Mon noon–3am, Tue–Sat 4pm–3am, Sun 4pm–midnight 🚋 City Circle Tram

HER MAJESTY'S THEATRE

This lovely old theatre, built in 1866, is one of Melbourne's leading locations for musicals and other major theatrical productions.

➕ F5 ✉ 219 Exhibition Street ☎ 8643 3300 🚋 City Circle Tram

JAMES SQUIRE BREWHOUSE

This micro-brewery serves the entire range of James Squire beers and also offers an extensive selection of cocktails and popular wines.

➕ A6 ✉ 439 Docklands Drive, Waterfront City ☎ 9600 0700 🕐 Noon–late 🚋 City Circle Tram

LAST LAUGH COMEDY CLUB

Enjoy a dinner show on Friday and Saturday nights, featuring professional local and international stand-up acts.

➕ F6 ✉ Athenaeum Theatre, 188 Collins Street ☎ 9650 6668 🕐 Fri–Sat 7pm–11pm 🚋 39, 109, 112

MELBOURNE TOWN HALL

A major site of choral and

orchestral performances, with occasional free Sunday concerts.

 E6 ✉ Swanston Street ☎ 9658 9779 🚋 City Circle Tram

PRINCESS THEATRE

Melbourne's most glorious performance space, in one of the city's finest buildings, is home to musicals and other leading theatrical events.

🔲 G5 ✉ 163 Spring Street ☎ 9299 9800 🚋 City Circle Tram

THE REGENT THEATRE

Opened in 1929 as a picture palace, the Regent is now equipped for both stage and screen and includes the dramatic Spanish rococo Plaza Ballroom.

🔲 F6 ✉ 191 Collins Street ☎ 9299 9800 🚋 City Circle Tram

TELSTRA DOME

This new super-stadium was designed for a variety of sports, including Australian Rules football and cricket, as well as concerts.

🔲 A6 ✉ Docklands ☎ 8625 7700 🎫 Call for details 🚋 City Circle Tram

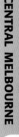

Restaurants

PRICES

Prices are approximate, based on a 3-course meal for one person.
$ A$10–A$20
$$ A$21–A$44
$$$ A$45–A$90

ARRIVERDERCI AROMA ($)

Italian-style café serving pasta and the like with good, strong coffee.

🔲 D5 ✉ 408 Queen Street ☎ 9606 0530 🎫 Breakfast, lunch and dinner Mon–Sat 🚋 City Circle Tram

BAR LOURINHA ($)

Casual modern tapas bar. Try the delicious stuffed squid and spicy rabbit and olive *empanadillas*.

🔲 F5 ✉ 37 Little Collins Street ☎ 9663 7890 🎫 Lunch Mon–Fri, dinner Mon–Sat 🚋 31, 109, 112

BECCO ($)

Trendsetters favour this elegant restaurant with its modern Italian fare.

🔲 E6 ✉ 11–25 Crossley Street ☎ 9663 3000 🎫 Lunch Mon–Fri, dinner daily 🚋 Tram 86, 96

CHINE ON PARAMOUNT ($$$)

This is a typical Chinese

ASIAN RESTAURANTS

Chinese restaurants were the main source of Asian cuisine in Melbourne for many years. Now the best of Chinese cuisine has achieved a superb level, and it is being joined by refined cuisine from Indonesia, Burma, Taiwan, Korea, Laos and other Asian countries. Most are reasonably priced and many are BYO.

restaurant where you will find authentic dishes in fine style.

🔲 F5 ✉ 101 Little Bourke Street ☎ 9663 6556 🎫 Lunch Mon–Sat, dinner daily 🚋 City Circle Tram

CITY WINE SHOP ($$)

You can purchase your wine from the shop to enjoy with a quick European-style meal, or choose from a wide range of wines by the glass.

🔲 G4 ✉ 161 Spring Crossley Street ☎ 9654 6657 🎫 Lunch and dinner daily 🚋 City Circle Tram

EUROPEAN ($$–$$$)

A city favourite, with French and Italian dishes, perfect ambience and great service.

🔲 G4 ✉ 161 Spring Street ☎ 9654 0811 🎫 Breakfast, lunch and dinner daily 🚋 City Circle Tram

FIFTEEN ($$$)

One of the Fifteen 'family', started by chef Jamie Oliver. Italian-inspired dishes using top-quality seasonal produce from all over Victoria.
✚ F6 ✉ 115–117 Collins Street (enter through George's Parade) ☎ 1300 799 415 ⏲ Lunch Mon–Sun, dinner Mon–Sat 🚃 31, 109, 112

FLOWER DRUM ($$$)

Melbourne's best Chinese restaurant offers Cantonese and other regional food in stylish surroundings.
✚ F5 ✉ 17 Market Lane ☎ 9662 3655 ⏲ Lunch Mon–Sat, dinner daily 🚃 City Circle Tram

GROSSI FLORENTINO ($$$)

One of Melbourne's oldest and best restaurants, with traditional European fare. Elegant; hard to beat.
✚ F5 ✉ 80 Bourke Street ☎ 9662 1811 ⏲ Lunch Mon–Fri, dinner Mon–Sat 🚃 City Circle Tram

HAIRY CANARY ($–$$$)

This trendy place is noisy and not for an intimate dinner for two, but the modern Mediterranean fare is inspired.
✚ E6 ✉ 212 Little Collins Street ☎ 9654 2471 ⏲ Breakfast Mon–Sat, lunch and dinner daily 🚃 City Circle Tram

HOFBRAUHAUS ($$)

Bavarian hospitality, live music and slap dancing, and tasty, hearty, traditional German cuisine.
✚ G5 ✉ 18–24 Market Lane ☎ 9663 3361 ⏲ Lunch Sun–Fri, dinner daily 🚃 86, 96

KUNI'S ($$)

This friendly Japanese restaurant, one of Melbourne's best, has a sushi bar as well as a main dining area.
✚ G5 ✉ 56 Little Bourke Street ☎ 9663 72431 ⏲ Lunch and dinner daily 🚃 86, 96

MASK OF CHINA ($$$)

This stylish, well-established restaurant, one of Melbourne's best,

---

EATING OUT

It has been said that you can eat your way around the world in Melbourne, and with more than 5,000 restaurants, the city may well be Australia's culinary capital. Immigrants have always influenced local tastes. In the past, Europeans set the standards, but today it is Asian chefs, more particularly Vietnamese and Thai, who are affecting what people eat. Restaurants are either licensed or BYO—bring your own alcoholic beverages. Most have a non-smoking area and some have banned smoking entirely. The best option for smokers is to check if smoking is allowed when making a reservation.

---

specializes in the food of Guangzhou province.
✚ F5 ✉ 115 Little Bourke Street ☎ 9663 7319 ⏲ Lunch Sun–Fri, dinner daily 🚃 City Circle Tram

MELBOURNE OYSTER BAR ($$$)

Oysters are the specialty, but fish and other seafood are presented in many ways. The giant seafood platters are popular.
✚ C6 ✉ 209 King Street ☎ 9670 1881 ⏲ Dinner Mon–Sat 🚃 City Circle Tram

PELLEGRINI'S ESPRESSO BAR ($)

A Melbourne institution, Pellegrini's is a classic Italian coffee bar offering excellent espresso and large helpings of minestrone, pastas and salads.
✚ F5 ✉ 66 Bourke Street ☎ 9662 1885 ⏲ Breakfast, lunch and dinner daily 🚃 Tram 85, 95, 96

TSINDOS ($$)

Traditional Greek cuisine and a welcoming family atmosphere. The menu includes grilled octopus, moussaka, lamb on the spit and seafood.
✚ E5 ✉ 197 Lonsdale Street ☎ 9663 3194 ⏲ Lunch Mon–Fri, dinner daily 🚃 Any Swanston Street tram

WARUNG AGUS ($$)

A long menu of Indonesian dishes in a Balinese setting.
✚ C3 ✉ 305 Victoria Street ☎ 9329 1737 ⏲ Dinner Tue–Sat 🚃 Tram 16

Accessible by the free City Circle Tram, and centred on the dramatic Federation Square, the area around Flinders Street has some of Melbourne's top attractions and pleasant riverside walks.

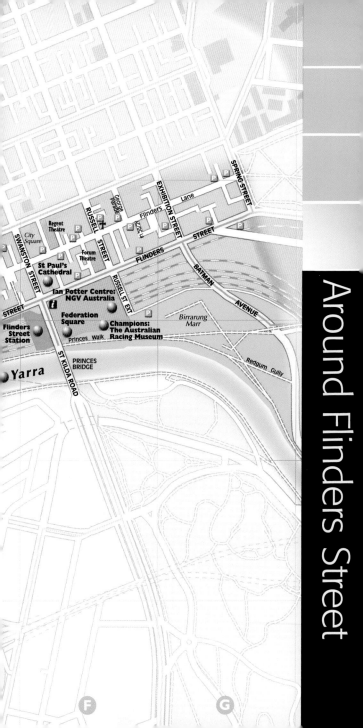

Regent
Theatre

City
Square

SWANSTON STREET

St Paul's
Cathedral

Ian Potter Centre:
NGV Australia

Flinders
Street
Station

Federation
Square

Yarra

RUSSELL STREET

Forum
Theatre

George Parade

EXHIBITION STREET

SPRING STREET

Lane

Flinders
Acacia

FLINDERS   STREET

RUSSELL ST EXT

BATMAN   AVENUE

Birrarung
Marr

Princes Walk

Champions:
The Australian
Racing Museum

Redgum Gully

ST KILDA ROAD

PRINCES
BRIDGE

STREET

F

G

Federation Square

HIGHLIGHTS

● Ian Potter Centre:
NGV Australia
● National Design Centre
● Centre for the Moving
Image
● Australian Racing Museum
● Daily guided tours
● Saturday Book Market
● Free concerts at BMW
Edge

TIP

● Make your first stop the
visitor centre and ask about
the free concerts held here.

Federation Square, billed as Melbourne's meeting place, has a mix of attractions, including the Ian Potter Centre and the Australian Centre for the Moving Image, along with 15 restaurants, cafés and bars.

What's on? There's usually something interesting happening in this huge complex, which covers a full city block. Built over an old railway yard, Fed Square (as it is known locally) was conceived as a civic heart for the city, and has enough museums, galleries, free attractions and places to dine to keep you busy for at least half a day. The Melbourne Visitor Centre is a must for information on what to see and where to stay. The BMW Edge, a 450-seat indoor amphitheatre, often stages free theatre, comedy, talks and presentations, and cabaret.

The futuristic Federation Square is dominated by high-rise office buildings (far left); the square is a popular gathering place for students (below); the fragmented designs of the cultural buildings are reflected on the inside (bottom left); there's no shortage of watering holes in the square (bottom right)

Cultural square While the prime attraction is the excellent Ian Potter Centre: NGV Australia (▷ 44), the high-tech galleries, cinemas and studio spaces of the Australian Centre for the Moving Image will give you the low-down on everything from more than a century of film history to the latest computer games and digital art. The National Design Centre showcases Australian design.

Green spaces Champions: The Australian Racing Museum (▷ 50) presents a history of Australian thoroughbred horse racing and includes a hall of fame. The adjacent Birrarung Marr, Melbourne's newest major park, lies on the north bank of the Yarra River and provides a link between the CBD and Melbourne's main sporting precinct. This contemporary park is part of a continuous green belt of parkland around the city.

THE BASICS

www.fedsquare.com
✚ F7
✉ Corner of Flinders and Swanston streets
🕐 All hours, various times for museums. Visitor centre daily 9–6
🍴 Cafés, restaurants and bars
🚆 Flinders Street
🚋 City Circle Tram
♿ Good
💲 Public areas free; admission to attractions

43

Ian Potter Centre: NGV Australia

TOP 25

The interior space of this superb gallery is almost as good as the collection itself

THE BASICS

www.ngv.vic.gov.au
➕ F6
✉ Federation Square
☎ 8620 2222
🕐 Tue–Sun 10–5 (Thu till 9pm)
🍴 Crossbart Café
Ⓡ Flinders Street
🚊 City Circle Tram; 48, 70, 75
♿ Good
💲 Free; charge for special exhibitions
❓ Good audio tours. The 'Icons of Australian art' tour gives a great introduction to Australian art

HIGHLIGHTS

● Aboriginal art
● Temporary exhibitions
● Tom Roberts' iconic *Shearing of the Rams*
● Emily Kngwarreye's classic work *Big Yam Dreaming*

The best place to see the world's largest collection of Australian art, plus special exhibitions, this stunning gallery has superb collections of indigenous and non-indigenous art from the colonial period to the present day.

Indigenous art The Ian Potter Centre houses a collection of great depth and complexity. On display in 20 galleries over three levels, the collection of Australian art from the colonial period through to contemporary art, includes Aboriginal and Torres Strait Islander art, photography, prints and drawings, fashion and textiles, and decorative arts. There are over 800 works (from its collection of 20,000) displayed at any one time. The 19th-century section contains works by the Heidelberg School artists such as Arthur Streeton, and includes Tom Roberts' *Shearing of the Rams*. From the 20th century are works by Margaret Preston, Arthur Boyd, John Brack and Fred Williams. The Indigenous Art section contains works by William Barak, Ginger Riley and Lin Onus. It also includes Emily Kngwarreye's classic work *Big Yam Dreaming*.

Room with a view The building is worth visiting in its own right. The interior spaces have been cleverly designed with shifting gallery view lines and cross connections giving a massive open feel. Contrasting this are enclosed calmer and darker galleries. Other sections are designed to open onto the landscape, with views across the Yarra River to the south.

On board ship at the Immigration Museum (left); displays at the museum (right)

TOP 25 **Immigration Museum**

Voices, images, letters and artefacts bring Victoria's immigration history to life in this contemporary museum. The former Customs Service building, renovated in the late 1990s, houses both the Hellenic Antiquities and Immigration museums.

Hardships revisited In this innovative museum special exhibitions sensitively explore themes of departure and arrival, journeys and settlement, and document the effects of immigration on Victoria since the early 1800s. Here you can walk through the re-creation of several ships' cabins and experience the cramped quarters endured by immigrants from the 1850s onwards on their way to Victoria. The Sarah and Baillieu Myer Immigration Discovery Centre has a library that focuses on cultural heritage and immigration, where you can look up information on family history. Outside, at the rear of the museum, is the Tribute Garden, a memorial courtyard bearing the names of immigrants. It's worth a visit for the building alone, which was built between 1858 and 1870. The centrepiece of the museum is the elegant Long Room, a marvellous piece of Renaissance revival architecture, featuring 16 Ionic columns and a mosaic tile floor.

Station Pier This Melbourne landmark is of iconic significance in Victoria's immigration history and is one of Australia's longest-operating passenger piers. The exhibition gallery on the second floor provides an historical overview of a migrant's arrival and the start of their new life in Australia.

THE BASICS

www.immigration.museum.vic.gov.au
🔢 D7
✉ 400 Flinders Street
☎ 9927 2700
🕐 Daily 10–5
🍴 Licensed café
🚇 Spencer Street or Flinders Street
🚋 City Circle Tram
♿ Good
🔆 Moderate

HIGHLIGHTS

● 'Ship' experience
● The Long Room
● The Tribute Garden
● Immigration Discovery Centre

AROUND FLINDERS STREET

TOP 25

Melbourne Aquarium

HIGHLIGHTS

- Hand-feeding the sharks
- Mangrove and billabong exhibits
- Simulator rides
- Deep sea trench
- Themed retail outlet
- Dive school
- Walk-through tunnels

TIP

- The aquarium can be crowded on school holidays and weekends.

This popular CBD attraction includes a walk-through view of life under the southern oceans and a chance to watch divers hand-feeding sharks and rays. If you're feeling adventurous, join them in the Dive with Sharks programme.

The aquarium Start your visit on the ground floor, where a multitude of tanks feature the smaller marine creatures of the world's oceans. In this area, a huge floor-to-ceiling tank, complete with coral atoll, contains many Great Barrier Reef invertebrates and fish. After a break at the Moorings Café, you can proceed to the first floor for a close look at the rays and fish in the re-created mangrove ecosystem, and the long-necked turtles and eels in the billabong. The rock pool exhibit, also on this level, has hermit crabs,

Fabulous sights—a giant ray at the Melbourne Aquarium (left); the waterside setting is home to one of the most popular attractions in the city (below); in the basement of the aquarium is the fascinating oceanarium, giving you a fish-eye's view of an amazing underwater world (bottom)

sea urchins, starfish, sea cucumbers and other creatures that can be handled. And in the Creepy Cave, you'll see pythons, leeches, bird-eating spiders, scorpions, giant cockroaches and stick insects, and giant Japanese spider crabs—huge!

The oceanarium For an insight into the diverse inhabitants of the Great Southern Ocean, walk down to the oceanarium, beneath the ground floor. Here you can walk along see-through tunnels, surrounded by a diverse array of sharks and rays, and talk to divers as they feed the fascinating inhabitants.

Action stations For an even more exhilarating experience, board one of the three state-of-the-art rollercoaster simulators. Or try the Dive with Sharks programme, if you dare.

THE BASICS

www.melbourneaquarium.com.au

🚼 D7

✉ Corner of Flinders and King streets

☎ 9620 0999

🕐 Daily 9.30–6

🍴 Snack bar and licensed brasserie

🚇 Spencer Street or Flinders Street

🚋 City Circle Tram

♿ Very good

💰 Moderate

❓ Glass bottom boat tours, special sessions for children/tour groups. Shop

The Yarra River

Central to the city is the beautiful Yarra River—take a boat trip for great views

THE BASICS

+ E7
✉ Melbourne River Cruises, Princes Walk
☎ 9629 7233; www.melbcruises.com.au
🕐 Daily
🚇 Various
💷 Walkways: free. Boat tours: moderate

HIGHLIGHTS

● The walkways
● View from the Princes Bridge
● Picnic spots
● River cruises
● Cycleways
● Studley Park Boathouse
● Cruising restaurant
● City lights at night

Because of its murky colour, the winding Yarra is known as the river that flows upside down. To the locals, the river is the heart and soul of the city. The waterway is perfect for a relaxing cruise.

The river The Yarra is not particularly busy along the city centre but you will often see tour boats cruising past and rowers practising their sport. However, there's plenty going on where the river empties into Port Phillip Bay and a good place to absorb the scene is from the Princes Bridge, built in 1888. The best thing to do is to take a tour boat.

The cruises The down-river cruise meanders past the city CBD and Southbank, along the historical Victoria Docks, and on to the exciting new Docklands residential, commercial and retail development. You can see Melbourne's lovely parks and gardens, as well as the stylish suburban architecture along the riverbanks. The Royal Botanic Gardens (▷ 60–61), Herring Island, Melbourne Olympic Park and the Melbourne Cricket Ground (▷ 74) are highlights of this trip. There are also combination tours, and alfresco dining aboard *The Spirit of Melbourne*.

Riverside Rent a bicycle in Alexandra Gardens and cycle up or down the river on the excellent bicycle paths. Picnics on the grassy banks of the Yarra are a Melbourne tradition. To see the Yarra in a natural setting, don't miss Studley Park Boathouse at Kew, 6.5km (4 miles) from the city, where you can rent rowing boats and canoes.

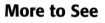

More to See

CHAMPIONS: THE AUSTRALIAN RACING MUSEUM

Showcasing Australia's thoroughbred racing industry and its role in Australia's cultural and sporting history, this comprehensive little museum is packed with interesting displays and racing memorabilia. Check out the lives of the owners, trainers and jockeys. The museum has a Hall of Fame dedicated to Australia's top racehorses.

✚ F7 ✉ Yarra Building, Federation Square ☎ 1300 1139 407 ⊙ Daily 10–5 ⊜ Flinders Street 🚊 City Circle Tram ⬇ Good 🎫 Free

RIALTO TOWERS

The observation deck on the 55th floor here provides spectacular 360-degree views. On a clear day you can see out over Port Phillip Bay and northwest to Tullamarine Airport. The café is a good place to warm up after the chilly winds on the outdoor decks. A visit to the deck after dark is a magical experience.

✚ D7 ✉ 525 Collins Street ☎ 9629 8222 ⊙ Sun–Thu 10–10, Fri–Sat 10–11

🍴 Licensed café ⊜ Flinders Street, Spencer Street ⬇ Good 🎫 Moderate

ST. PAUL'S CATHEDRAL

With its lofty spires and towers, beautiful stonework and magnificent stained glass, this Anglican cathedral is a classic example of Gothic revival architecture from the late 19th century. Inside you will see carved cedar woodwork, tessellated tiled floors and detailed, banded stonework.

✚ F6 ✉ Corner of Swanston and Flinders streets ☎ 9650 3791 ⊙ Daily 🚊 City Circle Tram 🎫 Free

VICTORIA POLICE MUSEUM

An integral part of the Police Historical Unit, this museum preserves old police records, photographs and artefacts from the 1800s. The museum reflects the diversity of work carried out by Victoria Police since the department was established in 1854 and displays period crime paraphernalia.

✚ C7 ✉ Galleria level, 637 Flinders Street ☎ 9247 5213 ⊙ Mon–Fri 10–4 🚊 City Circle Tram 🎫 Free

Night view from Rialto Towers observation deck

St. Paul's Cathedral on the edge of Federation Square

Shopping

ANGUS & ROBERTSON BOOKWORLD

A good selection of current titles plus several bins of discounted books.
➕ E6 ✉ Corner of Bourke and Elizabeth streets ☎ 9670 8861 🚋 City Circle Tram

BOBBY'S CUTS

This quirky guys' clothing shop presents its street-style clothing and artist-made accessories in old deli cabinets. Labels include American Apparel.
➕ E6 ✉ 4/237 Flinders Lane ☎ 9663 4030 🚋 City Circle Tram

CITY HATTERS

An Akubra hat from this shop provides good protection from the harsh sun.
➕ E7 ✉ 211 Flinders Street ☎ 9614 3294 🚋 City Circle Tram

KOKO BLACK

Only premium grade cacao is used for their range of hand-made chocolate products; favourites include Ice Cream Martini. Delicious pralines, coffees, teas and hot chocolate are all available at this popular shop.
➕ E7 ✉ Shop 4, Royal Arcade ☎ 9639 8911 🚋 City Circle Tram

Entertainment and Nightlife

CRUISING RESTAURANT

Board the *Spirit of Melbourne* for a dinner cruise featuring international cuisine and fine Australian wines.
➕ F7 ✉ Vault 11, Banana Alley, Flinders Street ☎ 8610 2600 🕙 Departs 7.30pm Fri and Sat 🚋 City Circle Tram

FORUM

Originally a picture palace, the Forum retains its dramatic interior but now hosts concerts and other events.
➕ F6 ✉ Corner of Flinders and Russell streets ☎ 9299 9800 🚋 City Circle Tram

THE PURPLE EMERALD

Groovy and retro, with live jazz and blues.
➕ E6 ✉ 191 Flinders Lane ☎ 9650 7753 🕙 Nightly, Wed–Sun 🚋 City Circle Tram

RIVERLAND BAR AND CAFÉ

Stunning river views, a great wine list, a variety of draught beers from around the world, plus an interesting menu and organic sausages on the barbecue.
➕ E6 ✉ Vault 1, Federation Wharf ☎ 9662 1771 🕙 Daily 7am–late 🚋 City Circle Tram

TRANSPORT HOTEL

One of Melbourne's favourite new pubs. Live music and DJs every night, 10 screens and big match events.
➕ F6 ✉ Corner of Princes Bridge and Northbank ☎ 9654 8808 🕙 Daily 11am–late 🚇 Flinders Street

YOUNG AND JACKSON'S

The city's most famous pub and the location of the stunning nude *Chloe*, a painting that shocked the city in the late 19th century.
➕ F6 ✉ 1 Swanston Street ☎ 9650 3884 🕙 Daily 🚋 City Circle Tram

---

THEATRE OFFERINGS

Australian theatre nurtured international stars such as Mel Gibson, Cate Blanchett, Geoffrey Rush and Toni Collette. You'll get a chance to see the stars of the future as well as view all kinds of dramatic entertainment at The Arts Centre (▷ 56), but look for performances by smaller theatre companies at The Malthouse and La Mama Theatre. Lavish hit musical productions are performed at grand old venues such as the Princess Theatre (▷ 37).

Restaurants

PRICES

Prices are approximate, based on a 3-course meal for one person.

$	A$10–A$20
$$	A$21–A$44
$$$	A$45–A$90

ARINTJI ($$)

This restaurant has spectacular city and river views and something for all tastes—drinks, light meals, tapas or à la carte menu. Great cocktails and wine by the glass. The changeable menu often includes a delicious whole deep-fried snapper with Thai three-flavoured sauce and succulent green pawpaw salad.
➕ F6 ✉ Yarra Building, Federation Square ☎ 9663 9900 Ⓒ Daily 10am–late 🚋 City Circle Tram

BLAKES ($$$)

The chef at this Melbourne institution, where Asia meets the Mediterranean, is not afraid to experiment. The modern decor and cool ambience are an added bonus.
➕ E7 ✉ Southgate, Southbank (short walk from city centre) ☎ 9682 6516 Ⓒ Lunch and dinner daily

BLUE TRAIN CAFÉ ($)

A really popular place, with tasty pizzas cooked in wood-fired ovens, and other light fare—and waiters who clearly enjoy their work.
➕ E7 ✉ Mid-level, Southgate Complex, Southbank (short walk from the city centre) ☎ 9696 0111 Ⓒ Breakfast, lunch and dinner daily

BOKCHOY TANG ($$)

Dine on contemporary Northern Chinese cuisine made with organic produce and where freshness and respect for the delicate, natural flavours

TRAMCAR RESTAURANT

One of Melbourne's dining institutions, the burgundy Colonial Tramcar Restaurants have been plying the streets of Melbourne for nearly 25 years. The first travelling tramcar restaurants in the world, they carry 36 diners per tram and have a set charge which includes three courses, cheeses and Australian wines. Dishes are predominantly Modern Australian cuisine and include grilled kangaroo loin and salmon mousse. Be sure to book well ahead. Dietary requirements must be advised no later than 24 hours in advance.
➕ D8 ✉ Departs from Tramstop 125 Normanby Road, near corner of Clarendon Street (near Crown Casino) ☎ 9696 4000; www.tramrestaurant.co.au Ⓒ Lunch and dinner daily

of each ingredient are paramount. Panoramic views of the city.
➕ F6 ✉ Level 3. The Crossbar, Federation Square ☎ 9650 8666 Ⓒ Daily 11.30am–late 🚋 City Circle Tram

CAFÉ CHINOTTO ($)

This small café serves reasonably priced pizza, pasta and salads, with rapid and friendly service. Set on two levels, one looking out onto the Square and the other opening onto the BMW Edge. Perfect for a coffee or lunch break between the sightseeing and the shopping.
➕ F6 ✉ Federation Square ☎ 9650 8666 Ⓒ Daily 10am–late 🚋 City Circle Tram

KENZAN ($$)

Exceptional sushi and sashimi—one of the largest selections in the city—and excellent service in elegant surroundings make this place very popular with both locals and tourists.
➕ G5 ✉ Collins Place, 56 Flinders Lane ☎ 9654 8933 Ⓒ Lunch Mon–Fri, dinner Mon–Sat 🚋 City Circle Tram

MECCA ($$–$$$)

Diners flock to this stylish place for the menu of dishes inspired by the cuisine of the Middle East.
➕ E7 ✉ Mid-level, Southgate, Southbank (short walk from city centre) ☎ 9682 2999 Ⓒ Lunch and dinner daily

Across the Princes Bridge are the leafy Royal Botanic Gardens, some fashionable suburbs and the entertainment precinct of Southbank, which includes the Crown Entertainment Complex, Southgate and the Arts Centre.

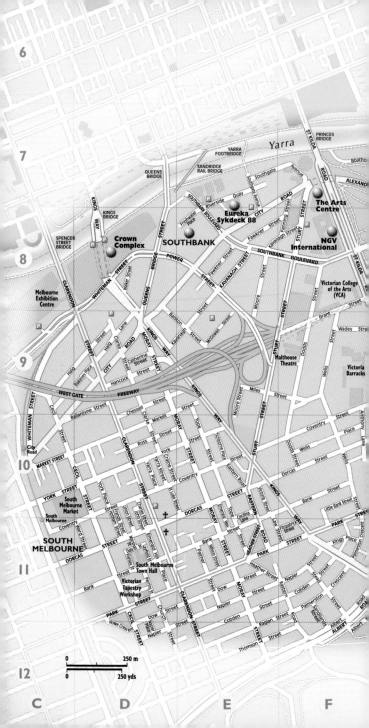

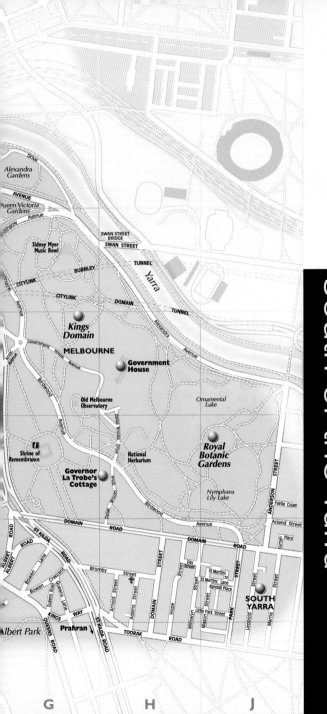

Alexandra
Gardens

Drive

AVENUE

Queen Victoria
Gardens

Avenue

SWAN STREET
BRIDGE

SWAN STREET

SWAN STREET

TUNNEL

Sidney Myer
Music Bowl

BURNLEY

Yarra

CITYLINK

CITYLINK

DOMAIN

TUNNEL

Kings
Domain

Avenue

MELBOURNE

Government
House

Birdwood

Government House Avenue

Old Melbourne
Observatory

Ornamental
Lake

Anderson Street Road

Shrine of
Remembrance

Avenue

National
Herbarium

Royal
Botanic
Gardens

ANDERSON STREET

Governor
La Trobe's
Cottage

Dallas Brooks Drive

Birdwood

Nymphaea
Lily Lake

Fairlie Court

Avenue

Acland street

DOMAIN

ROAD

DOMAIN

ROAD

Murphy Place

ROAD

ST KILDA

ROAD

Bromby

ROAD

Street

Day
Street

Street

Street

St Martins
Lane

St Martins
Lane

Randall Place

ALBERT ROAD

Bowen Lane

Queens Lane

Bowen

Crescent

Arnold Street

Adams Street

DOMAIN STREET

Hope Street

Millswn Street

Little Park Street

Mason Street

PARK STREET

Leopold Street

Marne Street

Street

SOUTH
YARRA

KINGS

QUEENS ROAD

Albert Park

WAY

Prahran

ST KILDA ROAD

TOORAK

ROAD

TOORAK

ROAD

G

H

J

The Arts Centre

TOP 25

Dominated by its elegant spire, the Arts Centre complex sits proudly by the river

THE BASICS

www.theartscentre.net.au

➕ F7

✉ 100 St. Kilda Road

☎ Information: 9281 8000. Ticketmaster: 1300 136 166

◐ Daily 7–late

🍴 Cafés and bars

🚊 Tram 3, 5, 6, 8

♿ Good

🎟 Free

❓ Guided tours daily, exhibitions, special tours and events. Check local press for current shows

HIGHLIGHTS

- Elegant spire
- Location on the Yarra River
- Concert Hall
- Artworks
- Theatres Building
- Performing Arts Museum
- Guided tours

The city's bastion of high culture is dominated by the webbed spire of the Theatres Building. The Hamer Hall, the State Theatre, the Playhouse and the Fairfax Studio are all part of The Arts Centre.

The Hamer This circular building next to the Yarra River is the city's main performing arts venue and home of the Melbourne Symphony Orchestra and the Australian Chamber Orchestra. The hall features a lavish interior, and a large collection of Australian art, and draws performers from around the world.

Theatres Building Linked to the Melbourne Hamer Hall by a walkway, this building houses the Playhouse, the State Theatre and the Fairfax Studio. The State Theatre features the world's largest mechanical stage. Overlooking the Yarra, next to EQ Cafébar, is BlackBox, an avant garde experimental space. Interesting and changing exhibitions of theatre costumes, set designs and other memorabilia are held in the Centre foyers. The George Adams Gallery, the major exhibition space, adjacent to the St. Kilda Road entrance, has exhibitions that complement The Arts Centre's performance programme. The Playhouse Theatre foyers house a stunning collection of Western Desert paintings by important indigenous artists.

Sidney Myer Music Bowl This popular, outdoor summer venue, set in the nearby Kings Domain Gardens, hosts everything from rock concerts to opera soloists.

The huge Eureka Tower is topped by the Skydeck, for amazing views of the city

Eureka Skydeck 88

Adjacent to the Yarra River, on the 88th level of the Eureka Tower, this observation deck includes a dramatic viewing experience in an extendable glass cube. It is Melbourne's tallest building at 300m (984ft).

What a view While waiting for the high-speed elevators to take you up, examine the 6m (20ft) multi-user, interactive 'Serendipity Table' that explores the stories and history of Melbourne. Once on the Skydeck, you are presented with a variety of viewing options. Besides the multi-directional glassed-in viewing sectors, there's a caged zone, 'The Terrace', where you can brave the outside elements.

Close to The Edge An additional thrill is available, if you choose to purchase a ticket for 'The Edge'— a 3m (10ft) square glass-cube that slides 3m (10ft) out from the building when it has its quota of brave souls on board. It's a weird sensation to be suspended 300m (698ft) above the ground and you can buy a souvenir photo to record your bravery. In poor weather conditions and high wind speeds, The Edge may not be operational. The SkyCafé serves drinks, snacks and light meals; the gift shop has souvenirs and gifts.

Statistics Eureka Skydeck 88 was completed in 2006, taking four years to build at a cost of A$500 million. The 13 lifts, the fastest in the Southern Hemisphere, travel at more than 9m (30ft) per second. The top of the building can flex up to 600mm (2ft) in high winds.

THE BASICS

www.eurekaskydeck.com.au

🔢 E7

✉ Riverside Quay, Southbank

☎ 9693 8888

🕐 Daily 10–10

🍴 Café

🚊 Flinders Street

♿ Good

💡 Skydeck: expensive. The Edge: moderate

HIGHLIGHTS

- Serendipity Table
- The Edge
- The Terrace
- Fine views

TIP

- Forget The Edge if heights worry you.

HIGHLIGHTS

- Asian art
- Dutch masters
- European art
- Sculpture courtyard
- Great Hall ceiling
- Decorative arts

TIP

- The stained-glass ceiling of the Great Hall is best viewed by lying on your back.

Australia's foremost art gallery has a vast collection of superb international art. The collections of the NGV are regarded as the most comprehensive in Australia, and some of the works are up there with the best in the world.

International collection This much-loved local icon, designed by Sir Roy Grounds in the early 1960s, was once home to an extensive collection of Australian and international art, but recently the NGV International has morphed into a gallery that features international art only. The gallery has more than 80,000 works of art, dating from 2,400bc to the present day, including Pre-Columbian artefacts, Greek and Roman antiquities, and a good collection of American paintings and sculpture. European Old Masters include Tiepolo,

Exterior and interior views of the NGV International, which contains one of the greatest collections of international art in the world

Rubens and Rembrandt, and there are also works by Rodin, Picasso, Monet, Van Gogh and Henry Moore. Photography, prints, costumes, textiles and decorative arts from all periods are represented by exquisite examples, presented in elegant and dramatic surroundings. Particularly worth looking out for is the Leonard French stained-glass ceiling of the Great Hall and the Asian art galleries.

Temporary exhibitions NGV International's diverse programme of special exhibitions, in conjunction with national and international art museums, brings in works of exceptional artists from around the world. The information desk has details of the lectures, floor talks, tours, films and children's activities on offer from time to time. Audio tours of the permanent and special exhibitions are available, for a gold coin donation.

THE BASICS

www.ngv.vic.gov.au
➕ F8
✉ 180 St. Kilda Road
☎ 9208 0222
🕐 Wed–Mon 10–5
🍴 Restaurant and café
🚃 Tram 3, 5, 6, 8
♿ Excellent
🎟 Free (charges for some exhibitions)
❓ Free tours daily, lectures, films, library and shop

Royal Botanic Gardens

TOP 25

- Visitor centre
- Plants in season
- Tree ferns
- Guided walks
- Ornamental lake
- Species names
- Riverside walk
- Observatory Café

TIP

The gardens are best visited in the early morning during the summer months.

One of the world's finest botanic gardens, this is a pleasant place to be on a hot summer's day, when you feel like some early morning exercise or a break from the city's bustle. Check out the free guided tours and open-air performances.

The gardens Established in 1846 by the famous botanist Baron von Mueller, these world-acclaimed gardens, covering about 36ha (89 acres), were superbly landscaped by William Guilfoyle, who created them in the 18th-century English tradition with rolling lawns, formal flower gardens and wooded coppices. Today more than 12,000 plant species from around the world are in all stages of bud and blossom at any given time. From June to August the camellias are at their best. Between September and November roses, azaleas and rhododendrons

Take a break from the busy city at the beautiful Royal Botanic Gardens

bloom. On a summer's day, Fern Gully is a cool, tranquil spot, with a resident colony of flying foxes resting in the trees. Don't miss the Australian rainforest section, where many species are identified.

Observatory Gate This entrance to the gardens is the ideal orientation point for your visit. At the visitor centre you can book a guided tour, browse the gardens, shop for unusual gifts and souvenirs, and enjoy breakfast, lunch or a snack in the excellent Observatory Café.

Aboriginal Heritage Walks On these walks, guides share their knowledge of the area and the life of the Bunurong and Woiwurrung people, custodians of the Melbourne area before Europeans arrived. You'll learn about their culture, their use of local plants and their history.

THE BASICS

➕ J10
✉ Birdwood Avenue
☎ Recorded message, after hours: 9252 2300. Aboriginal Heritage Walks: 9252 2300
🕐 Gardens: Apr–Oct daily 7.30am–6pm; Nov–Mar daily 7.30am–8pm. Aboriginal Heritage Walks: Thu, alternate Sun 11am
🍴 Observatory Café
🚊 Tram 8 to Stop 21
♿ Excellent
👐 Free
❓ Guided tours available

Southbank and the Crown Complex

This is the place for the latest in entertainment, dining and nightlife

THE BASICS

➕ E8 (Southbank);
D8 (Crown Complex)
✉ Crown Entertainment
Complex, Southbank
☎ 9292 8888
🕐 Casino Complex:
24 hours daily
🍴 Cafés and restaurants
🚉 Flinders Street
🚋 Tram 10, 12, 96, 109
🚤 Boat tours on the Yarra
♿ Moderate
🎟 Free
❓ Guided tours, night
viewing and exhibitions

HIGHLIGHTS

● River promenade
● Public art
● Shopping
● Cinemas
● Nightclubs
● Casino
● Restaurants
● Sunday market

Melburnians come here in great numbers on weekends to stroll along the Yarra River, shop, dine at restaurants offering choices of cuisine, and try their luck at the nearby Crown Casino.

Southbank This riverside district across from the city centre was once a dingy industrial area covered with warehouses and workshops. Since its redevelopment, it has become a popular spot for shopping and dining. Many of Melbourne's new attractions are located here, alongside the long-established Arts Centre and NGV International. Large sculptures line the riverbank and an arched footbridge joins the Southbank complex to the city. On Sundays the international food hall and an arts and crafts market draw the crowds.

Crown Complex Cinemas, cafés, cabarets and nightclubs make the Crown Entertainment Complex—to give it its full name—lively, especially on weekends. There are also 17 bars and 35 restaurants with a range of cuisines and many specialist shops. At night, the five-storey Atrium features a 90-minute, continuous Four Seasons light-and-sound show, incorporating three large, computerized fountains. Along the promenade, eight columns that overflow with water by day shoot fireballs at night.

Crown Casino Try your luck at pontoon, roulette, poker, pai gow and the Australian favourite, two-up. There are 350 gaming tables and 2,500 gaming machines in nine separate areas.

GOVERNMENT HOUSE

Set within quiet gardens, with the city skyline visible above the trees, this mansion was built in 1876 as the official residence of the Governor of Victoria. The interior is magnificently furnished and the ballroom is larger than the one at Buckingham Palace in London.

➕ H9 ✉ Dallas Brooks Drive ☎ Tours: 9656 9800 🕐 Mon, Wed, Sat 10am, 1pm 🍴 Observatory Gate Café 🚋 Tram 8 ✋ Moderate

GOVERNOR LA TROBE'S COTTAGE

This pretty little cottage, Victoria's first Government House, was brought from England in 1839 by Charles La Trobe, who became the first Lieutenant-Governor of the young colony. First set up at Jolimont, the building has been relocated and restored by Australia's National Trust, and many of the furnishings are original.

➕ H10 ✉ St. Kilda Road ☎ 9654 5528 🕐 Daily 11–4 🚋 Tram 3, 5, 6, 8 ♿ Good ✋ Free

KINGS DOMAIN

A major urban green space, the Kings Domain is also home to the Sidney Myer Music Bowl, the cottage of the first governor of Victoria, and the impressive Shrine of Remembrance, a memorial to those who died in World War I. The Alexandra Gardens and Queen Victoria Gardens adjoin the outstanding 36ha (89-acre) Royal Botanic Gardens, and together form a continuous park between Princes Bridge and South Yarra. Features include monuments to Queen Victoria and King George V.

➕ G9 ✉ St. Kilda Road ☎ 9654 5528 🕐 Daily 10–5 🚋 Tram 3, 5, 6, 8 ♿ Good ✋ Free

SOUTH YARRA AND PRAHRAN

One of the city's smartest areas, with its designer clothing, antiques, fine art, classy restaurants and people-watching. Explore Toorak Road and Chapel Street to get a sense of the place.

➕ J11/H12 and off map ✉ Toorak Road/Chapel Street 🍴 Many cafés, restaurants 🚋 Tram 8, 72

Governor La Trobe's cottage

Take a break at the Ay Oriental Tea House in Chapel Street, South Yarra

Domestic Architecture Walk

Melbourne's architectural heritage includes examples of elaborate ironwork, bluestone façades and decorative brickwork.

DISTANCE: 5km (3 miles)   **ALLOW:** 2 hours

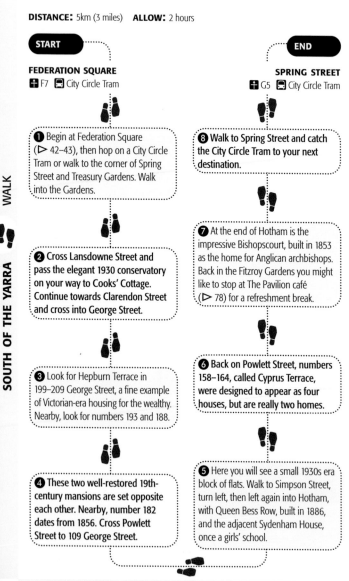

START

FEDERATION SQUARE
🔲 F7 🚋 City Circle Tram

END

SPRING STREET
🔲 G5 🚋 City Circle Tram

❶ Begin at Federation Square (▷ 42–43), then hop on a City Circle Tram or walk to the corner of Spring Street and Treasury Gardens. Walk into the Gardens.

❽ Walk to Spring Street and catch the City Circle Tram to your next destination.

❷ Cross Lansdowne Street and pass the elegant 1930 conservatory on your way to Cooks' Cottage. Continue towards Clarendon Street and cross into George Street.

❼ At the end of Hotham is the impressive Bishopscourt, built in 1853 as the home for Anglican archbishops. Back in the Fitzroy Gardens you might like to stop at The Pavilion café (▷ 78) for a refreshment break.

❸ Look for Hepburn Terrace in 199–209 George Street, a fine example of Victorian-era housing for the wealthy. Nearby, look for numbers 193 and 188.

❻ Back on Powlett Street, numbers 158–164, called Cyprus Terrace, were designed to appear as four houses, but are really two homes.

❹ These two well-restored 19th-century mansions are set opposite each other. Nearby, number 182 dates from 1856. Cross Powlett Street to 109 George Street.

❺ Here you will see a small 1930s era block of flats. Walk to Simpson Street, turn left, then left again into Hotham, with Queen Bess Row, built in 1886, and the adjacent Sydenham House, once a girls' school.

Shopping

ARTS CENTRE SHOP
Offers an excellent selection of arts-related merchandise, showcasing works by Australian artists and talented craftspeople, along with a range of inexpensive gifts.
✚ F7 ✉ 100 St. Kilda Road ☎ 9281 8285 🚊 Tram 3, 5

BORDERS
Melbourne's largest and most comprehensive book stockists, with a very large range of travel publications.
✚ Off map ✉ 500 Chapel Street, South Yarra ☎ 9824 2299 🚊 Trams 78, 79

DAKOTA 501
Boutique denim retailer specializing in quality local and international denim labels including Levis, Lee, Diesel, Adidas, 2K and Autonomy. All the top names.
✚ Off map ✉ 501 Chapel Street, South Yarra ☎ 9826 9596 🚊 Trams 78, 79

DESERT GEMS
Handmade jewellery from top Australian craftspeople.
✚ E7 ✉ Shop U9, Southgate (short walk from city centre) ☎ 9696 8211

ELIZABETH'S
Worth seeking out for its unique range of Melbourne-made jewellery in gold, silver and gemstones.
✚ E7 ✉ Shop M2, Southgate (short walk from city centre) ☎ 9696 7944

EMIL'S SHOE REPAIR
Handbags, vintage boots, belts and sheepskins.
✚ Off map ✉ 153 Chapel Street, Windsor ☎ 9521 1175 🚊 Trams 78, 79

EN ROUTE
The city's leading specialist shop for luggage stocks briefcases, handbags, wallets and backpacks.
✚ Off map ✉ 280 Toorak Road, South Yarra ☎ 9827 4709 🚊 Tram 8

FLAVOURS, HERBS & SPICES
Their own range of gourmet herbs and spices, dressings and spice blends, as well as lots of foodie gift ideas.
✚ Off map ✉ 113 Chapel Street, Windsor ☎ 9521 3288 🚊 Trams 78, 79

GREVILLE STREET MARKET
Appropriately sited on a hip and trendy street, this

UP-MARKET SHOPS
Shops at the upper end of Collins Street, and in South Yarra and Toorak, sell international designer labels. Other international shops include Fabergé, Gucci and Tiffany's at the Crown Entertainment Complex, (▷ 62) and the Galleria Plaza shops. For fine jewellery fashioned from Australian pearls, opals, gold or diamonds, visit one of the jewellery shops.

market sells retro goods and things alternative.
✚ Off map ✉ Greville Street, Prahran 🕐 Sun 12–5 🚊 Tram 78, 79

JAM FACTORY
Home to the huge Borders bookshop, a cinema complex, food outlets and many specialist shops, this former jam factory is a destination in its own right.
✚ Off map ✉ 500 Chapel Street, South Yarra 🚊 Tram 8

KAISERMAN
Individually designed pieces of jewellery, plus top brand-name watches.
✚ Off map ✉ 586 Chapel Street, South Yarra ☎ 9824 1088 🚊 Tram 78, 79

KEN DUNCAN GALLERY
Outstanding images of Australian landscapes by one of the world's leading exponents of panoramic photography.
✚ E7 ✉ Shop U6, Southgate (short walk from city centre) ☎ 9686 8022

KIRRA AUSTRALIA GALLERY
Fine Australian gifts, sculpture and decorative arts designed and hand-crafted in Australia.
✚ E7 ✉ Shop M7, Southgate (short walk from city centre) ☎ 9682 7923

MARY MARTIN BOOKSHOP
This stylish shop is a delightful place to

browse. There's an excellent Australiana section.
🏢 E7 ✉ Shop G18, Southgate, Southbank (short walk from city centre) ☎ 9699 2292 🕐 Daily 9–5

MIDDLE EIGHT MUSIC
One of Australia's top show-music stores. Has a wide range of CDs featuring jazz, cabaret, comedy and nostalgia.
🏢 Off map ✉ 144 Osborne Street, South Yarra 🚃 Tram 8

PRAHRAN MARKET
This lively favourite, a short walk from Chapel Street, sells fresh produce and delicatessen goods.
🏢 Off map ✉ 163–185 Commercial Road ☎ 9682 7923 🕐 Tue and Thu 10–5, Fri 6–6, Sat 6–1 🚃 Tram 8, 72 to Chapel Street

QUEEN CLOTHING
Fresh, 'quietly quirky' women's fashions by local designer, Christine Boyle.
🏢 Off map ✉ 80 Chapel Street, Windsor ☎ 9529 3191 🚃 Trams 78, 79

SAKS
The latest trends and stylish pieces, straight from European designers—including labels Alysi, Yasmin Velloza and Non e Vero.
🏢 Off map ✉ 64 Toorak Road, South Yarra ☎ 9821 4888 🚃 Tram 8

SAVILL GALLERIES
Extensive stock of paintings for sale by some of the country's most prominent artists. Also offers regular catalogued exhibitions and advice for art collectors.
🏢 Off map ✉ 262 Toorak Road, South Yarra ☎ 9827 8366 🚃 Tram 8

SOUTHGATE
This collection of shops and restaurants with great river views lies just across the Yarra River from the city centre, between the arts complex and the Crown Entertainment Complex (▷ 62).
🏢 E7 ✉ Southbank (short walk from city centre)

SOUTH MELBOURNE
Stallholders at this market sell everything from fresh fruit and vegetables to delicatessen items and household goods.
🏢 C10 ✉ Corner of Cecil and York streets ☎ 9209 6295 🕐 Wed 8–2, Fri 8–6, Sat

---

GEMS AND JEWELLERY
Opals are the most popular gemstones sought out by visitors although you'll also find South Sea pearls, Argyle diamonds and original designs in Australian gold. Visit several shops to get an idea of the variety and price range before deciding on your purchase. Many shops have examples of rough stones and a few even have displays explaining the mining process. All are happy to answer questions.

---

and Sun 8–4 🏢 South Melbourne

SOUTH YARRA & PRAHRAN
The stylish clothing shops and trendy restaurants of Chapel Street and Toorak Road attract those who come to see and be seen. Retro design and a gay subculture reign on Greville Street and Commercial Road.
🏢 Off map ✉ Chapel Street and Toorak Road, South Yarra; Greville Street and Commercial Road, Prahran 🚃 Tram 6, 8, 72

THE SUNDAY ART MARKET
An essential stop for interesting and unusual handcrafted works in the cultural hub of Melbourne.
🏢 F7 ✉ The Arts Centre 🕐 Sun 10–6 🚃 Flinders Street

WALTER'S WINE BAR
Choose from hundreds of Australian wines, including older vintages, and a great array of food to eat in or take away.
🏢 E7 ✉ Shop UR1, Southgate, Southbank (short walk from city centre) ☎ 9690 9211

THE WORKSHOP
A very wide range of art, craft and hobby supplies, plus many workshops, including paper, mosaic and felting techniques.
🏢 Off map ✉ 312 Chapel Street, Prahan ☎ 9533 6800 🚃 Trams 78, 79

Entertainment and Nightlife

BAR CODE

This round-the-clock operation with the techno thumping away in the background is a popular spot. Latest video games.
⊞ D8 ✉ Crown Entertainment Complex, Southbank (short walk from city centre) ☎ 9873 3811 🕐 Nightly from 8pm

BRIDIE O'REILLY'S

This popular Irish hotel serves all the favourites from the old country, plus good music, typical Irish decor and furnishings, and friendly company.
⊞ Off map ✉ 462 Chapel Street, South Yarra ☎ 9827 7788 🕐 Mon–Wed 11–1am, Thu–Sat 11–3am 🚋 Tram 78, 79

CHASERS

The latest dance music, old favourites and requests.
⊞ Off map ✉ 386 Chapel Street, South Yarra ☎ 9827 7379 🕐 Nightly 🚋 Trams 78, 79

CLUB ODEON

Melbourne's live music home, with the city's top DJs spinning tunes from the 1970s, 80s and 90s.
⊞ D8 ✉ Level 3, Crown Entertainment Complex, Southbank ☎ 9682 1888 🕐 Nightly from 9pm

DIVA BAR

Gay pub with a wide selection of music, from stage shows to current releases. Occasional dancing on the bar.

⊞ Off map ✉ 153 Commercial Road, South Yarra ☎ 9826 9747 🕐 2pm–1am 🚋 Tram 78, 79

FIDEL'S CIGAR LOUNGE

Looking for that favourite cigar? Fidel's is sure to have it, plus drinks and lots of smoke.
⊞ D8 ✉ Crown Entertainment Complex, Southbank ☎ 9292 6885 🕐 Daily 🚇 Flinders Street 🚋 Tram 10, 12, 96, 109

HAMER HALL

This is the city's prime performing arts venue. Look for performances by Melbourne Opera Company, Melbourne Symphony Orchestra and the Australian Ballet.
⊞ F7 ✉ The Arts Centre, Southbank ☎ 9281 8000

CLASSICAL MELBOURNE

The Arts Centre offers excellent opera, ballet and classical music. The world-renowned Melbourne Symphony Orchestra, the Australian Ballet and Australian opera companies all perform here regularly. The Melbourne Theatre Company has a regular season of productions at the State Theatre, while the complex's Playhouse presents a variety of theatrical productions. Classical music concerts are also given at the Town Hall and the Conservatorium of Music.

🕐 Call for hall tours 🚇 Flinders Street 🚋 Tram 3, 5, 6, 8

MELBOURNE SPORTS AND AQUATIC CENTRE

A variety of swimming pools as well as a popular wave pool. Other sports include table tennis, basketball and volleyball.
⊞ Off map ✉ Albert Park Road, Albert Park ☎ 9926 1555 🕐 Mon–Fri 9am–10pm, Sat–Sun 8am–8pm 🚋 Tram 12

MERCURY LOUNGE

Great acoustics and live pub-style bands most nights. DJs keep the show moving and the small dance floor busy.
⊞ D8 ✉ Crown Entertainment Complex, Southbank ☎ 9292 5480 🕐 Nightly from 8pm

P J O'BRIENS

A boisterous and somewhat beery alternative to the standard high-tech venue. Faux Irish decor and live Irish music.
⊞ E7 ✉ Southgate Complex (short walk from city centre) ☎ 9686 5011 🕐 Nightly

STATE THEATRE

The home of the excellent Melbourne Theatre Company, this intimate theatre also hosts Melbourne Dance Company performances.
⊞ F7 ✉ The Arts Centre, Southbank ☎ 9281 8000 🕐 Shows: Mon–Sat 🚇 Flinders Street 🚋 Tram 3, 5, 6, 8

Restaurants

PRICES

Prices are approximate, based on a 3-course meal for one person.

$	A$10–A$20
$$	A$21–A$44
$$$	A$45–A$90

CAFFÈ E CUCINA ($$–$$$)

Long popular with the glitterati and deservedly so, since the Italian food here is always delicious.
➕ Off map ✉ 581 Chapel Street, South Yarra ☎ 9827 4139 🍴 Breakfast, lunch and dinner Mon–Sat 🚋 Tram 8

THE DECK ($)

This European-style brasserie overlooking the Yarra and the city skyline serves light meals and coffee.
➕ E7 ✉ Southgate, Southbank (short walk from city centre) ☎ 9699 9544 🍴 Lunch and dinner daily

FRANCE SOIR ($$–$$$)

Always popular, and deservedly so for the good classic French dishes and extensive and varied wine list.
➕ Off map ✉ 11 Toorak Road, South Yarra ☎ 9866 8569 🍴 Lunch and dinner daily 🚋 Tram 8

THE GROOVE TRAIN ($)

International, Mediterranean and Modern Australian cuisines, plus pizza, vegetarian dishes, soups and seafood served in a comfortable corporate atmosphere.
➕ D11 ✉ 332 Clarendon Street, South Melbourne ☎ 9699 6199 🍴 Mon–Thu 7.30am–10.30pm, Fri–Sat 7.30am–11.30pm 🚋 Tram 112

NEAR EAST ($$$)

The dedicated staff here has created a rare balance of East and West, with a range of Southeast Asian dishes in an elegant, modern setting. The emphasis is on fresh ingredients.
➕ Off map ✉ 254 Park Street, South Melbourne ☎ 9699 1900 🍴 Lunch Mon–Fri, dinner daily 🚋 Tram 1

THE POINT ($$$)

A great location in Albert Park and stylish surroundings draw crowds, as does the seasonal modern fare.
➕ Off map ✉ Aquatic Drive, Albert Park ☎ 9682 5566

DINNER ON THE YARRA

What better way to experience Melbourne at night than a dinner cruise on the Yarra River. You definitely don't go for the food–it's the scenery, featuring the city skyline and docklands, that's the major draw. Operators include Melbourne River Cruises (lunches and dinners ☎ 9614 1215), Southbank Cruises (dinner ☎ 9646 5677) and City River Cruises (☎ 9650 2214).

SCUSA MI ($$$)

Overlooking the Yarra River and the city skyline, this top Italian restaurant uses only the best ingredients in its limited menu, with terrific results.
➕ E7 ✉ Mid-level, Southgate, Southbank (short walk from city centre) ☎ 9699 4111 🍴 Lunch and dinner daily

SWEET BASIL ($$)

Modern Thai cooking keeps company with old favourites here.
➕ Off map ✉ 209 Commercial Road, South Yarra ☎ 9827 3390 🍴 Dinner Tue–Sun 🚋 Tram 72

VIET'S QUAN ($$)

Minimalist and modern, with little to distract you from the food, which is authentic and just about the best value in town. It is always best to make a reservation.
➕ Off map ✉ 300 Toorak Road, South Yarra ☎ 9827 4765 🍴 Lunch and dinner Mon–Sat 🚋 Tram 8

ZAMPELIS CAFÉ GRECO ($$)

A smart place that serves a great range of Greek delicacies for all three courses. Strictly no reservations.
➕ D8 ✉ Crown Entertainment Complex, Southbank (short walk from city centre) ☎ 9686 9733 🍴 Lunch and dinner daily

Fringed by the lovely Fitzroy and Treasury Gardens, attractions eastwards of the CBD include the famous Melbourne Cricket Ground. Here, too, is Richmond, one of Melbourne's oldest suburbs.

VICTORIA

**Eastern Hill
Fire Museum**

NICHOLSON STREET

Evelyn
Place

ALBERT

Yarra

4

5

6

7

8

| 0 | | 250 m |
| 0 | | 250 yds |

E   **F**   **G**

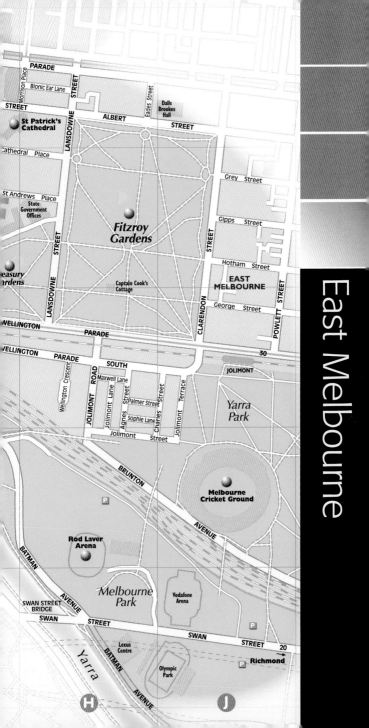

PARADE
Morrison Place
Bionic Ear Lane
STREET
St Patrick's Cathedral
Cathedral Place
St Andrews Place
State Government Offices
Treasury Gardens
LANSDOWNE STREET
STREET
ALBERT
Eades Street
Dalls Brookes Hall
STREET
Grey Street
Gipps Street
Hotham Street
EAST MELBOURNE
George Street
CLARENDON STREET
POWLETT STREET

Fitzroy Gardens

Captain Cook's Cottage

WELLINGTON PARADE

WELLINGTON PARADE
Wellington Crescent
ROAD
JOLIMONT
SOUTH
JOLIMONT
Maxwell Lane
Jolimont Lane
Agnes Street
Palmer Street
Sophie Lane
Charles Street
Jolimont Terrace
Jolimont Street
JOLIMONT
30
Yarra Park

BRUNTON
AVENUE
Melbourne Cricket Ground
P
Rod Laver Arena
BATMAN AVENUE
Melbourne Park
Vodafone Arena
P
SWAN STREET BRIDGE
SWAN STREET
SWAN STREET
20
Lexus Centre
Olympic Park
Richmond →
P
Yarra
BATMAN AVENUE

H   J

Relax in the gardens and visit Captain Cook's pretty English-style cottage

Fitzroy and Treasury Gardens

The magnificent, tree-lined avenues of the Fitzroy Gardens, designed in 1857, were laid out in the form of a Union Jack flag. A poignant memorial to former US President John F. Kennedy is the centre-piece of the nearby Treasury Gardens.

Fitzroy Gardens The Fitzroy Gardens, with partly hidden glades, waterfalls and shady avenues of elms forming canopies across the pathways, is the location of Cook's Cottage. Also within the gardens is the Fairy Tree, whose trunk is carved with fantasy figures and Australian animals, a conservatory and the miniature Tudor Village, which was presented to Melbourne by the people of Lambeth, London, in appreciation of food packages sent to Britain by Melburnians after World War II.

Cook's Cottage This small, typically English cottage, dating from 1755, was the home of the parents of the distinguished navigator, Captain James Cook. Dismantled, it was shipped from Yorkshire to Melbourne in 1934 to be erected, stone by stone, on this site in the Fitzroy Gardens. Furnished in the style of the period, it contains an interpretive area that explores the life of James Cook.

Treasury Gardens At lunchtime, many city work-ers frequent this pleasant, tranquil park planted with poplars, elms, oaks and cedars. There is a memorial to US President John F. Kennedy at the edge of the gardens' pretty ornamental lake.

THE BASICS

➕ H5 and G5
✉ Off Wellington Parade
☎ Cook's Cottage: 9658 8713
🕐 Cook's Cottage: daily 9–5.30
🍴 Restaurant
🚉 Jolimont
🚋 Tram 78, 79
♿ Moderate

HIGHLIGHTS

● Avenues of trees
● Conservatory
● Fairy Tree
● Model Tudor village
● Cook's Cottage
● John F. Kennedy Memorial

Melbourne Cricket Ground

Modern design meets traditional cricket at the Melbourne Cricket Ground

THE BASICS

www.mcg.org.au
🔲 J7
✉ Jolimont Street
☎ 9657 8879
🕐 Daily 10–3
🚋 Tram 48, 75
♿ Poor
💰 Moderate
❓ Tours depart hourly from the Gallery of Sport foyer, from 10–3 on non-event days

HIGHLIGHTS

● Standing on the playing field
● Members' Pavilion
● Interactive games
● Olympic Museum
● Australian Gallery of Sport

Many Melburnians live for sport, especially cricket and their beloved Australian Rules Football. This 100,000-seat arena has long been the epicentre of these two sports in the city and was the focal point of the 1956 Olympics.

The hallowed ground Each week of the season, football followers deck themselves out in their team colours and flock to the MCG. If you are in Melbourne, attend a football or cricket match and soak up the atmosphere—few stadiums in the world generate the excitement of the MCG. A guided tour is always a must: you can sit in the room where the team watches the game, visit the Long Room hung with portraits of cricketing greats, and inspect the memorabilia-packed Melbourne Cricket Club Museum. For many, a tour highlight is to stand on the famous playing field.

Olympic Museum This major International Olympic Committee-endorsed museum traces the history of the modern games. There are photographic displays of each of the modern Olympics, with priceless items of memorabilia such as wild olive branches won at Athens in 1896 and various gold medals.

Australian Gallery of Sport Perhaps the best way to learn about cricket and Australian Rules Football is to visit this gallery, in the same complex, which includes the Australian Cricket Hall of Fame and hosts temporary exhibitions.

More to See

EASTERN HILL FIRE MUSEUM
On the ground floor of a 19th-century fire station, this museum houses a collection of fire-fighting memorabilia such as uniforms and photographs, and including Australia's largest collection of restored fire trucks. The collection comprises the biggest amount of fire equipment in the southern hemisphere, spanning several hundred years.

➕ G4 ✉ 48 Gisborne Street
☎ 9662 2907 ⏰ Fri 9–3, Sun 10–4
🚌 Tram 109, 112 from Collins Street
✋ Inexpensive

RICHMOND
In Richmond, one of the city's oldest suburbs and only a short tram ride from the CBD, you can find fashion outlets, with designer seconds, and some great Greek food. Vietnamese culture thrives on Victoria Street, Melbourne's Little Saigon, with enticing aromas and exotic dishes.

➕ Off map at J8 ✉ Bridge Road, Swan Street and Victoria Street 🍴 Many cafés and restaurants 🚌 Tram 48, 75

ROD LAVER ARENA
One of Australia's largest sporting and entertainment venues, named after legendary Australian tennis player Rod Laver. Seating over 15,000, the arena attracts over 1.5 million visitors to events each year, including the annual prestigious Australian Open tennis event. The innovative moveable roof takes just 30 minutes to open or close.

➕ H7 ✉ Batman Avenue, Melbourne and Olympic Park precinct ☎ 132 849 (event bookings) ⏰ Events vary, call for information 🚉 Flinders Street 🚌 Tram 9, 12 from Flinders Street ✋ Expensive

ST. PATRICK'S CATHEDRAL
You can see the graceful spires of this bluestone Catholic cathedral, built in 1897, from many points in the city. The interior has soaring, slender pillars, large stained-glass windows and mosaic floor tiles. Exquisite glass mosaics, made in Venice, are set into the marble and alabaster altars.

➕ G4 ✉ Cathedral Place ☎ 9662 2233
⏰ Mon–Fri 7–6, Sat–Sun 8–7.30 🚌 Tram 9, 12 from Collins Street ✋ Free

Detail from the community project mural in Stephenson Street, Richmond

Shopping

BRANDS UNITED
This factory outlet sells predominantly clothing, plus men's and women's underwear and lingerie, including such top fashion brands as Bonds, Calvin Klein, Morrissey, Oroton, Kooki and Antz Pantz.
🔽 Off map ✉ 221 Bridge Road and Swan Street, Richmond ☎ 9427 8772 🚋 Tram 48, 75

RICHMOND
Apart from the suburb's Greek and Vietnamese shops, Bridge Road and Swan Street offer designer seconds outlets and other shopping experiences. It makes a pleasant change to get out of the city to this vibrant suburb.
🔽 Off map ✉ Bridge Road and Swan Street, Richmond 🚋 Tram 48, 70, 109

RICHMOND HILL CAFÉ AND LARDER
Food expert Stephanie Alexander's fine condiments and fresh produce are for sale here, as well as a huge selection of cheeses. They also have cheese night events. The place doubles as a café serving tasty, fresh meals.
🔽 Off map ✉ 48 Bridge Road, Richmond ☎ 9421 2808 🚋 Tram 75

Entertainment and Nightlife

BASKETBALL
Melbourne Park is the home of the NBL basketball teams, the Melbourne Tigers and the Melbourne Titans, who compete in the national competitions.
🔽 J8 ✉ Melbourne Park ☎ 9914 5133 ⏰ Oct–Apr usually Fri, Sat 🚋 Tram 70

CORNER HOTEL
Listen to a great range of cutting-edge music at this Melbourne institution with a changing line-up of bands.
🔽 Off map ✉ 57 Swan Street, Richmond ☎ 9427 9198 ⏰ Most nights 🚋 Tram 70

ROYAL OAK HOTEL
This traditional pub has a large-screen TV showing sporting events, and a small TAB (betting shop) means you can place a bet. A bistro has nightly specials, and offers well-priced meals.
🔽 Off map ✉ 527 Bridge Road, Richmond ☎ 9428

4200 ⏰ Daily 10am–late 🚋 Tram 45, 75

SPREAD EAGLE HOTEL
This vibrant, bustling corner pub, with 10 beer brands on tap, has live jazz on Saturdays, and a bistro specializing in traditional pub fare at reasonable prices.
🔽 Off map ✉ 372 Bridge Road, Richmond ☎ 9428 6895 ⏰ Daily 10am–late 🚋 Tram 45, 75

THE SWAN HOTEL
A traditional pub, the perfect venue to enjoy live music. Serves great Italian meals and has a spacious beer garden. Friday and Saturday nights feature an in-house DJ.
🔽 Off map ✉ 425 Church Street, Richmond ☎ 9428 2112 ⏰ Daily 11am–late 🚋 Tram 48, 7

Restaurants

PRICES

Prices are approximate, based on a 3-course meal for one person.

$	A$10–A$20
$$	A$21–A$44
$$$	A$45–A$90

BURMESE HOUSE ($$)

Burmese music in the background, an open kitchen in the middle, and friendly staff create an unforgettable atmosphere. Be sure to try the egg noodles and chicken coconut curry.
➕ Off map ✉ 303 Bridge road, Richmond ☎ 9421 2861 🕔 Lunch Wed–Fri 11.30–2.30, dinner daily 5.30–10 🚃 Tram 48, 70, 109

THE COMMUNE ($)

Popular as a casual lunch spot, with a delicious range of savoury pastries, baguettes and focaccias. Thursday night is steak and jazz night.
➕ Off map ✉ 2 Parliament Place, East Melbourne ☎ 9654 5477 🕔 Mon–Fri 7.30–5.30 🚃 Tram 109, 122

FENIX ($$$)

Outstanding riverside restaurant offering dishes composed of unusual ingredients for the adventurous, as well as steaks, grilled fish and salads.
➕ Off map ✉ 680 Victoria Street, Richmond ☎ 9427 8500 🕔 Tue–Sat 12–3, 6–10.30, Sat–Sun 8.30am–3pm 🚃 Tram 109

THE GATE ($$$)

This large and lively Vietnamese restaurant offers refined cuisine in an elegant setting, plus a variety of entertainment. Reservations advised.
➕ Off map ✉ 545 Church Street, Richmond ☎ 9428 5127 🕔 Lunch and dinner daily 🚃 Tram 78, 79

GEORGE STREET CAFÉ ($)

Tasty, hearty breakfasts and lunches with large servings and outside seating for warmer days. The Bircher muesli with fresh fruit salad is a breakfast special.
➕ Off map ✉ 65 George Street, East Melbourne ☎ 9419 5805 🕔 Mon–Fri 7–5, Sat–Sun 8–5 🚃 Tram 48, 75

MIN TAN II ($)

A huge menu of Chinese and Vietnamese dishes,

VICTORIAN WINES

Australian wines have come a long way in recent years and are now exported to Europe, the US and Asia in huge quantities. It's worth seeking out Victorian wines to go with your food, particularly those from the Yarra Valley. Varieties include Cabernet Sauvignon, Shiraz, Chardonnay and Chablis. Good winemakers to look for include De Bortoli, Best's, Yering Station and Diamond Valley.

with especially good seafood, makes this no-frills restaurant a favourite with discerning diners.
➕ Off map ✉ 190 Victoria Street, Richmond ☎ 9427 7131 🕔 Lunch and dinner daily 🚃 Tram 23, 42, 109

THE PAVILION ($)

Set in an ornamental garden in the magnificent Fitzroy Gardens, there is plenty of tasty café-style fare on offer here for breakfast and lunch daily.
➕ Off map ✉ Fitzroy Gardens, East Melbourne ☎ 9417 2544 🕔 Mon–Fri 7.30–3.30, Sat–Sun 8–4 🚃 Tram 23, 42, 109

RADII ($$)

Extravagant decor and high-class culinary creations. Here you can watch your meal being prepared in the open kitchen, from a menu of fresh, seasonal European dishes.
➕ Off map ✉ Park Hyatt Hotel 1, Parliament Square, East Melbourne ☎ 9224 1211 🕔 Lunch and dinner daily 🚃 Tram 23, 42, 109

RICHMOND HILL CAFÉ & LARDER ($$)

Contemporary, Mediterranean-style dishes, efficient service, plus an excellent cheese shop. Breakfast is served until 3pm.
➕ Off map ✉ 48–50 Bridge Road, Richmond ☎ 9428 5127 🕔 Daily 8.30–5 (until 6 Fri–Sat) 🚃 Tram 48, 70, 109

These lively inner-city suburbs are easily reached by tram from the CBD. Carlton, with its excellent museum, has good eateries, bookshops and galleries, while eclectic Fitzroy exudes an alternative atmosphere.

Carlton and Fitzroy

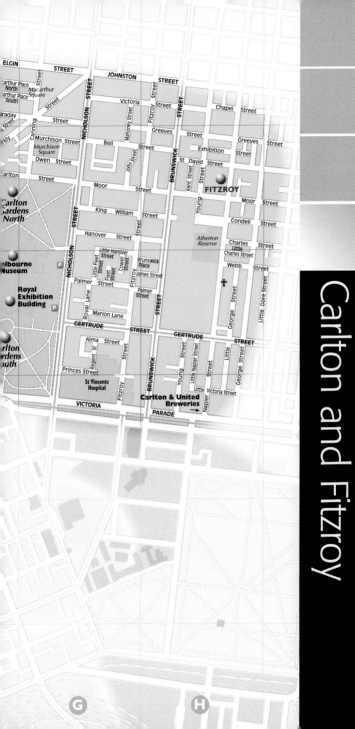

Carlton

Carlton is popular for eating out—Lygon Street (left) and University Café (right)

THE BASICS

🔲 E2
✉ Lygon Street, Rathdowne Street
🍴 Many cafés and restaurants
🚋 Tram 1, 22

HIGHLIGHTS

● Italian culture
● Restaurants
● Nightlife
● Specialty shopping

This trendy suburb, a ten-minute walk north of the CBD and close to Melbourne University, has long been dubbed the city's Little Italy. Its epicentre is bustling Lygon Street, with its alfresco dining scene.

Tasty Italian Carlton's Italian origins date from the early 1900s, when Italian migrants settled here, and were boosted with post World War II migration. It is the perfect near-city destination for a gastronomic expedition, since there are any number of excellent eating places to tempt you. In old double-storeyed Victorian terraced houses, restaurants literally spill onto the footpath, their colourful umbrellas providing shelter and busy waiters serving bowls of pasta and espressos to appreciative diners.

Lots to do Besides delicious Italian fare, you'll find boutiques, specialty men's and women's clothing shops of all descriptions, jewellery shops and gift and design shops on a leisurely stroll. Try to catch a performance at La Mama Theatre (▷ 89), one of Melbourne's original experimental theatres, where productions are often new works showcasing up-and-coming writers and actors.

More delights There are also art cinemas, bookshops and plenty of interesting galleries, and Lygon Street has one of the best bookshops in Melbourne, Readings (▷ 88). At the northern end of Argyle Street is Piazza Italia, with gardens, stone paving and a huge solar clock. Here you can sit in the sun, close your eyes, and dream of being in Italy.

Bohemian lifestyle and festival parades are central to the suburb of Fitzroy

Fitzroy

A casual walk along Fitzroy's lively Brunswick Street, with its fascinating people, quirky bazaars, excellent restaurants and exciting nightlife, provides a glimpse of an alternative Melbourne.

Multicultural Once a fashionable residential area, Fitzroy has since gone through phases of working-class and immigrant inhabitants. Today the area is increasingly occupied by some of Melbourne's vibrant subcultures, including students and artists, along with trendy, inner-city urbanites attracted by the suburb's eclectic nature. Part of the fun of hanging out here is to sit with a coffee and people-watch. For shopping, the area is hard to beat; it's a great place to buy books, art, antiques and the latest retro fashions. Melbourne's Spanish community is based in nearby Johnson Street, where you will find specialist eating places, grocery shops and gift shops. You'll also find food of every variety—Turkish, Greek, Italian, Thai, Malaysian and Tibetan—especially around the junction with Johnson Street. There are plenty of restaurants featuring modern Australian cuisine, too. For the best choice head for places with a crowd—the local stamp of approval.

Melbourne's art scene If you are interested in art, find your way to Gertrude Street, where Melbourne's emerging artists show their work. You'll also find some retro fashion and cutting-edge grunge clothing shops here, along with more hip coffee shops, where students from nearby Melbourne University hang out.

THE BASICS

➕ H2
✉ Brunswick Street
🍽 Cafés and restaurants
🚊 Tram 11
♿ Fair

HIGHLIGHTS

● People-watching
● Bric-a-brac shops
● Designer clothes shops
● Nightlife
● Art galleries

Melbourne Museum

Melbourne's Children's Museum (left); Aboriginal panels in the main museum (right)

THE BASICS

www.melbourne.museum.
vic.gov.au
⊞ F3
✉ Melbourne Museum,
Carlton Gardens, Carlton
☎ 13 11 02/8341 7777
🕔 Daily 10–5
🍴 Café and restaurant
🚋 City Circle Tram
♿ Excellent
💷 Moderate
❓ Guided tours

IMAX Theatre
✉ Rathdowne Street,
Carlton
☎ 9663 5454

HIGHLIGHTS

● Bunjilaka Aboriginal
Centre
● Decorative Arts section
● Children's Discovery
Centre
● IMAX cinema
● Forest Gallery
● Science Gallery

This ultra-modern museum features the art, culture and natural history of Melbourne and the surrounding area, using interaction, performance and the latest technology.

Museum exhibitions Major touring exhibitions supplement the collections of this museum in Carlton Gardens, opposite the grand 19th-century Royal Exhibition Building. The Bunjilaka Aboriginal Centre tells the stories of Victorian Aborigines, and explores the land and issues relating to Aboriginal laws, property and traditional knowledge. The People and Places Gallery focuses primarily on Melbourne's history.

Our world In the impressive Forest Gallery you walk among living trees, plants, animals, birds and insects; five interpretive zones explain the effects of fire, water, earth movement, climate and humans on the forests around Melbourne. Exhibitions in the Science Gallery show how much science shapes our world. Technology exhibitions explore the rapid evolution of digital technology and its dramatic effects on our daily lives. Check out the intricate workings of human beings in the popular Human Mind and Body Gallery.

Family fun Nearby at the Children's Museum, in a huge, colourful, cube-shaped building known as the Big Box, kids and their families are encouraged to engage with interactive exhibitions to learn about themselves. The IMAX cinema is in the complex, along with shops and cafés.

Placid giraffes, bathing elephants and lowland gorillas are just some of the creatures at the zoo

Melbourne Zoo

Gorillas get top billing here, but the otters are just as fascinating, as are kangaroos, koalas and wombats. The platypus is also represented, together with much of Australia's unique birdlife.

Background This popular zoo, the third oldest in the world, was established in 1862 on its present site in Royal Park. Back in the 1850s, Australian flora and fauna was famous for its diversity. The Acclimatisation Society was formed to gather and protect native species, and help them to adjust to captivity. This society merged with the Zoological Society in 1861 to create the zoo.

Australian fauna Today the zoo exhibits more than 350 animal species from around the world, most housed in landscaped enclosures. Platypuses caper in the nocturnal display and fur seals glide past in an underwater environment. Even the gorillas have their own rainforest. You can actually walk right through the lions' den. Sumatran tigers, otters and pygmy hippopotamuses star in the innovative African and Asian zones.

Royal Park The zoo is the focal point of this 180ha (445-acre) park. There are hockey and net-ball stadiums here, as well as facilities for cricket, football, tennis and golf. Elsewhere, green open spaces, shady roads, gardens of native plants and groves of smooth eucalyptus trees make you feel far away from busy Melbourne. Look for the memorial cairn to Burke and Wills, commemorating the fateful crossing of the Australian interior in 1860.

THE BASICS

www.zoo.org.au
➕ Off map at D1
✉ Elliot Avenue, Parkville
☎ 9285 9300
🕐 Daily 9–5
🍴 Variety of cafés and kiosks
🚋 Tram 55, 68, City Explorer Bus
♿ Good
💲 Moderate
❓ Guided tours, special zoo-keeper presentations and talks

HIGHLIGHTS

● Western lowland gorillas
● Sumatran tigers
● Australian mammals
● Butterfly House
● Japanese Garden
● Platypus nocturnal display
● Royal Park

CARLTON AND FITZROY

TOP 25

More to See

CARLTON AND UNITED BREWERIES

For a trip to an Australian brewery take a two-hour tour, departing from the Carlton Brewhouse that will include a look at the production, bottling and keg lines, before returning to the tasting room to sample different beers. You get a sample bag and there is a café for refreshments. Bookings are advisable.

⊞ Off map at H4 ✉ Corner of Nelson and Thompson streets, Abbotsford ☎ 9420 6800 🕐 Tours Mon–Fri at 10, 2 🚌 Tram 109 🖐 Expensive

CARLTON GARDENS

These gardens, also known as the Exhibition Gardens, are well laid out with public art, a huge fountain and avenues of mature trees. In the centre is the Royal Exhibition Building, built for the Great Exhibition of 1888, and still used for trade shows. Next to Carlton Gardens, in Nicholson Street, is a restored row of bluestone terraced houses, known as Royal Terrace. The innovative Melbourne Museum is next to the gardens to the north.

⊞ F2/F3 ✉ Between Rathdowne and Nicholson streets 🚋 City Circle Tram 🖐 Free

ROYAL EXHIBITION BUILDING

Listed on the UNESCO register of World Heritage buildings, this recently restored, magnificent old building was built for the International Exhibition of 1880 and remains the world's oldest surviving building of its type. The first Australian parliament met here in 1901.

⊞ F3 ✉ Nicholson Street, Carlton ☎ 1300 130 152 🕐 Tours daily at 2 🚌 Trams 86, 96 🖐 Inexpensive

UNIVERSITY OF MELBOURNE

Wander around these attractive grounds and admire the buildings, including Ormond College (1879), with its Gothic tower, and Newman College, designed in 1918 by Walter Burley Griffin, the architect responsible for Canberra, the purpose-built, administrative capital of Australia.

⊞ D1 ✉ Grattan Street, Parkville ☎ Media Office: 9344 4000 🕐 Daily 🍴 Several cafés 🚌 Tram 1, 3 🖐 Free

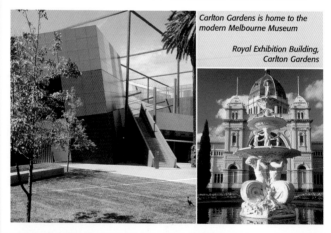

Carlton Gardens is home to the modern Melbourne Museum

Royal Exhibition Building, Carlton Gardens

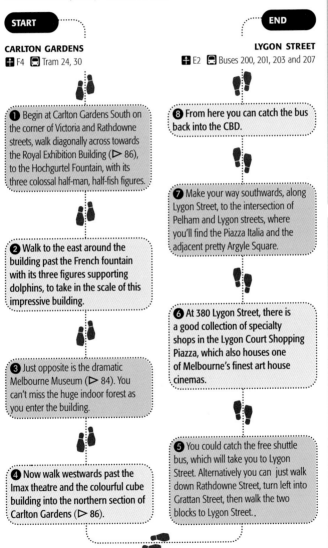

Carlton Gardens to Lygon Street

This interesting walk includes the grand old Royal Exhibition Building, the new Melbourne Museum and bustling Lygon Street.

DISTANCE: 3km (2 miles)　**ALLOW:** 3 hours

START

CARLTON GARDENS
⊞ F4　🚍 Tram 24, 30

END

LYGON STREET
⊞ E2　🚍 Buses 200, 201, 203 and 207

❶ Begin at Carlton Gardens South on the corner of Victoria and Rathdowne streets, walk diagonally across towards the Royal Exhibition Building (▷ 86), to the Hochgurtel Fountain, with its three colossal half-man, half-fish figures.

❷ Walk to the east around the building past the French fountain with its three figures supporting dolphins, to take in the scale of this impressive building.

❸ Just opposite is the dramatic Melbourne Museum (▷ 84). You can't miss the huge indoor forest as you enter the building.

❹ Now walk westwards past the Imax theatre and the colourful cube building into the northern section of Carlton Gardens (▷ 86).

❽ From here you can catch the bus back into the CBD.

❼ Make your way southwards, along Lygon Street, to the intersection of Pelham and Lygon streets, where you'll find the Piazza Italia and the adjacent pretty Argyle Square.

❻ At 380 Lygon Street, there is a good collection of specialty shops in the Lygon Court Shopping Piazza, which also houses one of Melbourne's finest art house cinemas.

❺ You could catch the free shuttle bus, which will take you to Lygon Street. Alternatively you can just walk down Rathdowne Street, turn left into Grattan Street, then walk the two blocks to Lygon Street.

Shopping

ALPHAVILLE
Sophisticated, quirky clothing for men and women.
➕ H1 ✉ 262 Brunswick Street, Fitzroy ☎ 9416 4296
🚋 Tram 112

BRUNSWICK STREET BOOKSTORE
This excellent, eclectic shop has all the latest titles and more, plus plenty of places to sit and read.
➕ H2 ✉ 305 Brunswick Street, Fitzroy ☎ 9416 1030
🚋 Tram 11

CARLTON
Follow your nose to delicious coffee and fresh pasta on Lygon Street, Melbourne's own Little Italy. Check out the great shopping in the surrounding area.
➕ E2 ✉ Lygon Street, Carlton 🚋 Tram 1, 22

CIRCA VINTAGE CLOTHING
Good quality antique and vintage clothing for men and women—1850 to 1975—all lovingly restored to their original glory. Also stocks some new reproductions.
➕ H3 ✉ Shop 1, 102 Gertrude Street, Fitzroy
🚋 Tram 86

DENIM DELUXE
Denim superstore—great range of street wear and skate wear, plus sale jeans and brand labels at reduced prices.
➕ J1 ✉ 4/397 Smith Street, Fitzroy ☎ 9486 9050
🚋 Tram 86

FITZROY
The way-out shops on Brunswick Street, the city's liveliest street, reflect the alternative nature of the suburb. Good for fashion, books and galleries.
➕ H2 ✉ Brunswick Street, Fitzroy 🚋 Tram 11, 86

ISHKA HANDCRAFTS
Handcrafts from developing communities globally—gifts, homeware, jewellery and furniture.
➕ G1 ✉ 300 Nicholson Street, Fitzroy ☎ 9416 07877
🚋 Tram 96

KUNDALINI RISING
Showcasing independent Melbourne designers—distinctive, exclusive, wearable clothing, plus jewellery and accessories.
➕ Off map ✉ 405 Brunswick Street, Fitzroy ☎ 9419 5294 🚋 Tram 112

MAKE DESIGNED OBJECTS
Quality local and internationally designed objects from Ittala, Rosendahl, Fink & Co!, Menu and Evasolo.

➕ E1 ✉ 194 Elgin Street, Carlton ☎ 9347 4225
🚋 Tram 1, 15

MONDO MUSIC
Specialist importer of Italian music, movies, T-shirts and gifts.
➕ E2 ✉ 211 Lygon Street, Carlton ☎ 1300 735 263
🚋 Tram 1, 8

MUSIC SWOP SHOP
Lots of second-hand musical instruments for sale, also custom instrument design and repairs.
➕ E1 ✉ 147 Elgin Street, Carlton ☎ 9348 1194
🚋 Tram 1, 15

THE ORIGINAL LOLLY SHOP
American, English and Dutch sweets, European chocolates, plus good old Australian favourites.
➕ E2 ✉ 239 Lygon Street, Carlton ☎ 9347 5641
🚋 Tram 1, 8

READINGS
One of Melbourne's top bookshops, which sells an excellent range of the latest titles and CDs.
➕ E2 ✉ 309 Lygon Street, Carlton ☎ 9347 6633
🚋 Tram 1, 22

TOMORROW NEVER KNOWS
Melbourne designers offer casual clothing for men and women, plus the coolest T-shirts in Melbourne.
➕ Off map ✉ 415 Brunswick Street, Fitzroy ☎ 9495 6645 🚋 Tram 112

Entertainment and Nightlife

CINEMA NOVA
This art house cinema complex offers top new-release art house and commercial films, special film festivals and events. Located in the Lygon Court Shopping Piazza.
✚ Off map ✉ 380 Lygon Street, Carlton ☎ 9347 5531 🚋 Tram 1, 8

COMICS LOUNGE
Australia's only live comedy venue that's open every night of the week. Seats 400, has two bars and a large dance floor.
✚ B2 ✉ 26 Errol Street, Melbourne ☎ 9348 9488 🚋 Tram 96

DAN O'CONNELL HOTEL
A warm and welcoming Irish atmosphere and live music seven days a week.
✚ G1 ✉ 225 Canning Street, Carlton ☎ 9347 1502 🚋 Tram 96

EMPRESS HOTEL
This cosy pub and popular live music venue hosts regular acoustic performances—mostly local bands and some touring acts.
✚ Off map ✉ 714 Nicholson Street, North Fitzroy ☎ 9489 8605 🚋 Tram 96

EVELYN HOTEL
A Fitzroy institution, this funky hotel has an out-door beer garden, live band music most nights, a front bar with a big screen and pool table—and reasonably priced drinks.
✚ H1 ✉ 351 Brunswick Street, Fitzroy ☎ 9419 5500 🕐 Daily 🚋 Tram 112

IMAX
The screens are the biggest in the world, the projectors and sound systems are state-of-the-art, and the movies are specially made to suit.
✚ F3 ✉ Melbourne Museum, Carlton ☎ 9663 5454 🚋 City Circle Tram

LA MAMA THEATRE
One of the city's principal venues for new theatre, showcasing Australian talent.
✚ F1 ✉ 205 Faraday Street, Carlton ☎ 9347 6142 🚋 Tram 96

PLANET AFRIK
Also known as Africa Bar. Relax at a bare wooden table with your safari

THE CINEMA SCENE
Melbourne's cinema scene is thriving. Of the many cinemas, the main complexes are on Bourke and Russell streets and at the Jam Factory and the Crown Entertainment Complex. More alternative cinemas include the Longford in South Yarra, the Kino at Collins Place and the Capital Theatre at 113 Swanston Street. For foreign and off-beat films try the Lumiere at 108 Lonsdale Street. Schedules are in *the Age* and *the Herald Sun*.

cocktail and enjoy the fantastic West African music. The club's menu includes hearty African dishes.
✚ J3 ✉ 99 Smith Street, Carlton ☎ 9419 2687 🕐 Daily 🚋 Tram 86

THE NIGHT CAT
This popular 1950s place spins rock 'n' roll on Wednesdays and cool jazz from Thursday to Sunday.
✚ H1 ✉ 141 Johnson Street, Fitzroy ☎ 9417 0090 🕐 Wed–Sun 8–1 🚋 Tram 11

THE PROVINCIAL HOTEL
One of Brunswick Street's most popular haunts serves great food, and a huge open fire adds atmosphere and keeps everyone warm in winter.
✚ H2 ✉ 299 Brunswick Street, Fitzroy ☎ 9417 2228 🕐 Daily 🚋 Tram 11

RAINBOW HOTEL
Cold beer and great bands are the primary attractions at this popular hotel.
✚ H2 ✉ 27 St. David Street, Fitzroy ☎ 9525 3599 🕐 Daily 🚋 Tram 11

ROYAL PARK
The perfect venue for walking, cycling, tennis, roller-blading and jogging. There are also facilities for golf, football and cricket.
✚ Off map ✉ Off Royal Parade, Parkville ☎ 9568 8713 🕐 Daily during daylight hours 🚋 Tram 19

CARLTON AND FITZROY

ENTERTAINMENT AND NIGHTLIFE

Restauraunts

PRICES

Prices are approximate, based on a 3-course meal for one person.

$	A$10–A$20
$$	A$21–A$44
$$$	A$45–A$90

CAFÉ DIONYSOS ($$–$$$)

A traditional Greek taverna with fresh seafood prepared in the Greek style.
🔲 E2 ✉ 139 Cardigan Street, Carlton ☎ 9347 8766 🕐 Lunch Mon–Fri, dinner Mon–Sat 🚋 Tram 1, 3, 22

JIMMY WATSON'S WINE BAR & RESTAURANT ($$)

This Melbourne institution is the place to socialize and sample wines of great quality. Check out the cellar.
🔲 F1 ✉ 333 Lygon Street, Carlton ☎ 9347 3985 🕐 Mon 12–6, Tue–Sat 12–10, Sun 12–4 🚋 Tram 96

LEMONGRASS ($$–$$$)

Some people call this Melbourne's best Thai restaurant. The food is creative and the setting restrained and elegant. Specializes in ancient royal Thai recipes.
🔲 E2 ✉ 174 Lygon Street, Carlton ☎ 9662 2244 🕐 Lunch Mon–Fri, dinner Wed–Sun 🚋 Tram 96

PENANG AFFAIR ($)

This Malaysian restaurant serves all the old favourites, including curries and *laksas* (a one-dish meal of rice noodles with either chicken or seafood).
🔲 H1 ✉ 325 Brunswick Street, Fitzroy ☎ 9419 7594 🕐 Lunch Tue–Fri, dinner daily 🚋 Tram 11

PIREAUS BLUES ($$)

This Greek restaurant, decorated with traditional objects from the homeland, is one of the city's more popular. Reservations essential.
🔲 H1 ✉ 310 Brunswick Street, Fitzroy ☎ 9417 0222 🕐 Lunch Wed–Fri and Sun, dinner daily 🚋 Tram 11

RATHDOWNE STREET FOOD STORE ($)

Well-prepared dishes, from pasta to curries, are available to take away.

THAI AND VIETNAMESE

Australians have turned to Thai food in a big way in the last 20 years and the quality of food in the best Thai restaurants in Sydney and Melbourne is equal to that anywhere outside Thailand—light and tasty, based on very fresh produce and delicate spices and herbs. Vietnamese cuisine now rivals Thai cuisine in popularity, especially in Melbourne, where many refugees settled after the war in their homeland. Pricey Vietnamese establishments with refined cuisine are proliferating.

🔲 F2 ✉ 617 Rathdowne Street, Carlton North ☎ 9347 4064 🕐 Mon–Sat 7am–11pm, Sun 7.30–5 🚋 Tram 96

RETRO CAFÉ

The name says it all. The food is good and hearty, and there are coffees for all moods.
🔲 H1 ✉ 413 Brunswick Street, Fitzroy ☎ 9419 9103 🕐 Breakfast, lunch and dinner daily 🚋 Tram 11

SUKHOTHAI ($)

The smart Thai surroundings, together with a great selection of traditional food, have earned this place a string of awards.
🔲 H1 ✉ 234 Johnston Street, Fitzroy ☎ 9419 4040 🕐 Dinner daily 🚋 Tram 11

THAI THANI ($$)

Locals have long known this place for its great selection of authentic food, served in ersatz Thai surroundings, at reasonable prices.
🔲 H1 ✉ 293 Brunswick Street, Fitzroy ☎ 9419 6463 🕐 Dinner daily 🚋 Tram 11

TOOFEY'S ($$)

One of the city's top seafood restaurants, this well-established place offers the freshest seafood cooked to perfection and a well-priced wine list.
🔲 F1 ✉ 162 Elgin Street, Carlton ☎ 9347 9838 🕐 Lunch Tue–Fri, dinner Tue–Sun 🚋 Tram 1, 22

Try to explore some of the city's outer sub-urbs and attractions a bit farther out. The city's seaside at St. Kilda is only 20 minutes by tram from the CBD, and a day trip on the Great Ocean Road is well worthwhile.

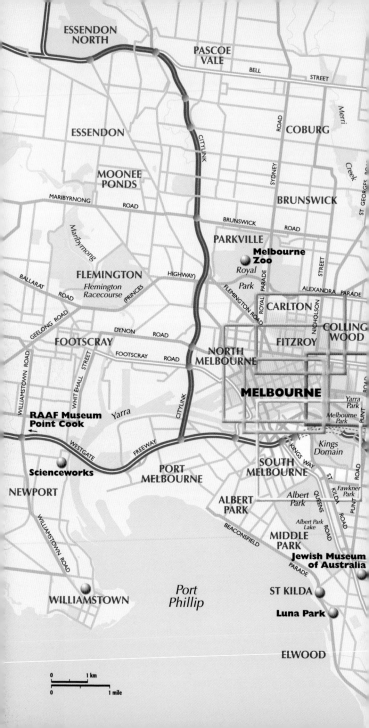

Heide Museum of Modern Art

TOP
25

Modern building and abstract sculpture reflecting the style of art found in the Heide

THE BASICS

www.heide.com.au

🟦 Off map to northeast

✉ 7 Templestowe Road, Bulleen

☎ Museum: 9850 1500. Café: 9852 2346

🕐 Tue–Fri 10–5, Sat–Sun 12–5

🍴 Café Tue–Sun 11–5

🚉 Heidelberg station

🚌 From station, take bus 291 and alight near the museum

♿ Good

💲 Moderate

❓ Audio tour

HIGHLIGHTS

● Contemporary art
● Audio tour
● Walks
● Sculpture garden
● Heide store

Celebrating the work of Australia's early modernists, this very special museum and its riverbank sculpture gardens were once the stomping ground of a new generation of artists, whose aim was nothing short of revolutionizing Australian art.

The gallery Set on the banks of the Yarra River, Heide first belonged to John and Sunday Reed, whose patronage, beginning in the 1930s, nurtured a new generation of outstanding artists. Starting with a run-down dairy farm, the Reeds built a fine contemporary home and created an inspiring environment in which artists could meet and work.

Modern art Today these buildings house a permanent collection of Australian modernists—paintings by Arthur Boyd, Charles Blackman, Joy Hester, Sidney Nolan, Albert Tucker, Peter Booth and Jenny Watson, and sculptures by Rick Amor and Stephen Killick. The Discover Heide audio tour provides insights into the lives of the artists influenced by the Reeds.

The garden Stroll around 5ha (12 acres) of parklands and picnic among the contemporary sculptures in the grounds and along the riverbank. The rambling park comprises native and European trees and has a well-tended kitchen garden and sculpture gardens running right down to the Yarra River. Or try the restaurant at the entrance to the museum. Temporary exhibitions and events offer perspectives on aspects of Australian art.

Rippon Lea and Como House

Managed by the National Trust, these outstanding examples of 19th-century suburban estates are just a few kilometres apart, south of the Yarra River. Their magnificent gardens are intact and their architecture is very well preserved.

Rippon Lea Built between 1868 and 1887 with distinctive polychrome bricks, this lavish, ornate, Romanesque mansion has 36 opulent rooms where Victorian splendour mixes with the 1930s tastes of its last owner. The fine 5.7ha (14 acres) Victorian pleasure garden includes an orchard, a desert garden, an ornamental lake with islands and decorative bridges, a 19th-century conservatory and a grand Victorian fernery. Be sure to bring a picnic lunch or have a coffee at the Gate House, then spend the afternoon touring the mansion and relaxing by the lake. Access to the house is by tour only, so book ahead.

Como House Two hectares (5 acres) of gardens surround this elegant home, built between 1840 and 1859, in an unusual mix of Australian Regency and Italianate styles. This gracious building perfectly exemplifies the wealthy landowner lifestyle in mid 19th-century Australia. The kitchen outbuilding dates from the 1840s, and the original laundry and some furnishings also remain. Sloping lawns, walks among flower gardens, and pine and cypress glades make up the grounds; there's also a croquet lawn, a fountain terrace and a water garden by 19th-century landscape designer Eliss Stones.

THE BASICS

Rippon Lea
➕ Off map to southeast
✉ 192 Hotham Street, Elsternwick
☎ 9523 6095
🕐 Daily 10–5
🚋 Tram 67
♿ Moderate
❓ Guided tours daily

Como House
➕ Off map to east
✉ Corner of Williams Road and Lechlade Avenue, South Yarra
☎ 9827 2500
🕐 Daily 10–5
🚋 Tram 8
♿ Moderate
❓ Guided tours daily

HIGHLIGHTS

● Unique architecture
● Original furniture
● Park-like grounds
● Fountain terrace
● Stunning interior decoration

FARTHER AFIELD

★

TOP 25

Sci120eworks

Hands-on and action packed—the exciting Scienceworks museum caters for all ages

HIGHLIGHTS

● Hands-on exhibits
● Planetarium shows
● Temporary exhibits
● Old steam pumps

Opened in 1992, this hands-on science and technology museum is an exciting showcase of science past, present and future. For a fast, digital trip around the universe, visit the adjacent Planetarium.

Exhibitions 'House Secrets' is highly interactive and shows the science behind many everyday items in our homes—our appliances, our pets and the food we eat. In the 'Nitty Gritty Super City' there's a construction zone, where you can explore science in the city—pedal a pianola, drive a digger and create your own buildings. At 'The Ultimate Challenge', try the extreme snowboarding experience and the 3-D soccer goalie game. Here you can discover your sporting talents and profile. The educational and interactive 'Muck Bunker Stormwater Experience' shows how you can stop Max Muck from polluting our waterways.

Planetarium In the only digital planetarium in the southern hemisphere, a great range of shows recreate the night sky and give you a close up look at the moon, the stars and our planets. The Planetarium has a 16m (52ft) domed ceiling, a stereo surround-sound system, and a new high-resolution video projection system that presents an unforgettable astronomical experience.

The Pumping Station One of Australia's most important industrial heritage sites, the station has giant working steam-driven pumps, now driven by compressed air. These were a key component of the city's first centralized sewerage system.

A stunning ariel view of St. Kilda, with the magical Luna Park at its heart

St. Kilda and Luna Park

TOP 25

Take a walk along the Esplanade and pier to work up an appetite for a meal in one of the area's many fine restaurants. For cakes and pastries, a visit to nearby Acland Street is a must.

The beach Since Melbourne's early days people have flocked to this beachside suburb, 6.5km (4 miles) southeast of the city, to enjoy the cool sea breezes off Port Phillip Bay. Late in the 19th century, the wealthy built large houses in the area, away from the heat of the city. The beaches are fine for swimming, although there can be an undertow. Windsurfing is popular.

The streets Now, post-gentrification, Fitzroy and Acland streets are a mix of retail and dining establishments, lively bars and art galleries. Many of the grand old buildings have been restored and the charm of the place is immense. On Sundays an open-air arts and crafts market along the Esplanade draws huge crowds.

St. Kilda Pier This popular pier, erected in 1857, is about 150m (164 yards) from the beach end of Fitzroy Street and two blocks northwest of Luna Park. From the café and marina at the end of the pier you can see the grand sweep of the bay around to Port Melbourne.

Luna Park Built in 1912, this St. Kilda institution is one of the oldest amusement parks in the world. The carousel that dates back to the park's earliest days remains a great favourite.

THE BASICS

St. Kilda
✚ Off map to south
☎ Visitor Information: 132 842
🕐 24 hours daily
🚌 Bus 16 from Swanston Street
♿ Generally good
✋ Free

Luna Park
www.lunapark.com.au
✚ Off map to south
☎ 9525 5033
🕐 Fri 7–11pm (summer only); Sat 11–11; Sun 11–6
🍴 Food stalls
🚊 Trams 16, 96
✋ Moderate

HIGHLIGHTS

● Swimming in summer
● Cafés on Fitzroy Street and Acland Street
● Patisseries
● Walking on the pier or along the beach
● St. Kilda Botanical Gardens
● Nightlife

FARTHER AFIELD

TOP 25

More to See

JEWISH MUSEUM OF AUSTRALIA

Dedicated to the conservation, preservation and exhibition of Jewish heritage, arts, customs and religious practices, this museum presents the Australian–Jewish experience. Permanent exhibitions use state-of-the-art interactive displays to explain the Jewish year, belief and ritual, and there's a timeline of Jewish history.
✚ Off map to south ✉ 26 Alma Road, St. Kilda ☎ 9534 0083 🕐 Tue–Thu 10–4, Sun 11–5 🚋 Tram 3, 67 💷 Inexpensive

MONTSALVAT

This amazing group of buildings was hand-crafted between 1934 and the 1970s, using mud brick, stone, hewn timbers and slate building materials recycled from some of Melbourne's fine old buildings. A working art colony of artists and craftspeople, who sell their works, is housed here.
✚ Off map to northeast ✉ Hillcrest Avenue, Eltham ☎ 9439 8771 🕐 Daily 9–5 🚆 To Eltham then take Woodridge bus 💷 Moderate

RAAF MUSEUM POINT COOK

Based at Point Cook, the birthplace of the Australian Flying Corps and the Royal Australian Air Force, this museum presents the history of the second-oldest air force in the world.
✚ Off map to west ✉ RAAF Base Williams, Point Cook Road, Point Cook ☎ 9748 5094 🕐 Tue–Fri 10–3, Sat–Sun 10–5. Interactive flying displays Tue, Thu, Sun 1 🚌 Werribee Park Shuttle daily to Point Cook 💷 Free

WILLIAMSTOWN

A visit to this bayside suburb, best reached by the Westgate Bridge or by a ferry from Southbank and seaside St. Kilda, makes a great day trip. Shipping docks, moored yachts and boat chandlers all contribute to the maritime atmosphere. Walk along the Strand to take in the arts and crafts shops, and check out the backstreets, with their clothing and gift shops, small restaurants and interesting old buildings.
✚ Off map to southwest ✉ The Strand, The Marina 🍴 Many cafés and restaurants 🚢 Southbank

City ferries at Williamstown

Open-air drinks break in Williamstown

Excursions

DANDENONG RANGES

The scenic Dandenongs have always been Melburnians' favoured summer recreation destination.

Soaring mountain ash forests, glades of tree ferns and mountain streams are all part of the experience in the Dandenongs. The highest point is Mount Dandenong at 633m (2,076ft). Besides hiking and picnicking, there are magnificent gardens, art and craft shops, nurseries and tearooms to visit. Along the southeastern slopes, on the edge of Sherbrooke Forest Park, the narrow-gauge Puffing Billy Railway carries day-trippers from quaint Belgrave, in the foothills, to pretty Emerald Lake Park in the mountains.

William Ricketts Sanctuary, set in a tranquil, 1.6ha (4-acre) wooded area, displays 200 half-hidden, kiln-fired, clay sculptures of Aboriginal figures, the work of the talented sculptor William Ricketts (1899–1993), who founded the sanctuary, nestled among mossy rocks and tree ferns.

THE BASICS

www.dandenongranges
tourism.com.au
Distance: 35km (22 miles)
east of the city
Journey Time: 45 minutes
🛈 Visitor Centre: 1211
Burwood Highway, Upper
Ferntree Gully ☎ 9758
7522 🕐 Daily 9–5
🚌 Bus 16 from Swanston
Street
♿ Poor
✋ Moderate

HEALESVILLE SANCTUARY

One of Australia's most highly regarded wildlife parks, Healesville is set in the foothills of the scenic Yarra Valley.

On display are more than 200 native species, including kangaroos, emus, koalas, wombats, dingoes and platypuses in surroundings as near natural as possible. You can learn about the animals from their keepers, as they go on their daily rounds. There are also walk-through aviaries, a wetlands walkway and a nocturnal house. See the working wildlife hospital where sick, injured and orphaned wildlife are cared for, and talk with the vets about native wildlife health. The Working Sanctuary Tour presents a behind-the-scenes look at the operations of Healesville, while the Burra Burra Yan Indigenous Walking Tour gives you an idea of Aboriginal traditions and culture.

THE BASICS

Distance: 60km (38 miles)
Journey Time: 1 hour
✉ Badger Creek Road,
Healesville
☎ 5957 2800
🕐 Daily 9–5
🍴 Café; picnic areas
🚌 Bus tour
✋ Expensive

GREAT OCEAN ROAD

Built by soldiers from World War I, and opened in 1932, the Great Ocean Road is one of the world's great scenic drives.

The journey from Torquay, southwest of Melbourne, to Warrnambool and beyond encompasses rainforests, seaside beach towns, cliff-edge roadways, forests and dramatic offshore rock formations. Past Torquay and nearby Bells Beach (regarded as Australia's surfing capital) is the popular and quaint seaside town of Lorne, and the nearby fishing port Apollo Bay. Near Port Campbell you encounter the famed Twelve Apostles, natural rock formations, weathered by the wind and water, standing in the ocean just offshore. Loch Ard Gorge, the site of a legendary shipwreck, can be reached by a walking trail. The Great Ocean Road is an excellent bus day tour, but could also be undertaken in a more leisurely way as a self-drive trip.

THE BASICS

www.greatoceanroad.org
Distance: 350km (220 miles)
Journey Time: 8 hours
🛈 Geelong and Great Ocean Road Visitor Centre
✉ Stead Park, Princes Highway, Corio ☎ 5275 5797
❓ Australian Pacific Touring ☎ 1300 655 9645

PHILLIP ISLAND

On the island's Summerland Beach you can view a colony of little penguins every night at the Penguin Parade.

Spotlights illuminate these engaging birds as around 4,500 of them return to their nesting burrows in the evening. There is commentary from an experienced ranger and a choice of viewing places, including the Penguin Sky Box, an elevated viewing tower. Bring warm clothing, as nights can be cold and the weather unpredictable. Phillip Island has a substantial waterbird population and there are elevated boardwalks through bushland allowing good viewing opportunities.

At the Koala Conservation Centre, located on Phillip Island Tourist Road, Cowes (tel 9277 855, daily 10–5, moderate), you can wander along treetop boardwalks and easily spot koalas, or walk the one-kilometre track around the centre, where there are signs pointing to koalas in trees.

THE BASICS

www.visitportphillipisland.com
Distance: 125km (80 miles)
Journey Time: 8 hours
🛈 Phillip Island Visitor Centre ✉ 896 Phillip Island Road, Newhaven ☎ 5956 7447 🕐 Daily 10–two hours after sunset. Penguin Parade every night after sunset
🍴 Restaurants; picnic areas
💲 Moderate to expensive
❓ Australian Pacific Touring ☎ 1300 655 9645

WERRIBEE MANSION AND OPEN RANGE ZOO

This renovated old mansion stands on the banks of the Werribee River, a 30-minute drive from the city, on the way to Geelong.

Here guides in period costume, and audio headphones, show this imposing, 19th-century example of Australia's pastoral heritage to its best advantage. Constructed between 1874 and 1877, the Italianate mansion, with its 10ha (25 acres) of formal grounds, bluestone farm buildings and orchard, is the largest private residence ever built in Victoria. Next to the mansion, the Victoria State Rose Garden has over 4,000 rose bushes. At the Open Range Zoo you can either stroll around the zoo's 200ha (494 acres) at your own pace, or take a 50-minute guided safari around the grassy plains and sweeping river terraces. Giraffes, zebra, antelope and hippos roam freely here. Walking tracks pass natural enclosures with cheetahs, monkeys and ostriches.

THE BASICS

Distance: 29km (18 miles)
Journey Time: 45 minutes
✉ The Mansion at Werribee, Open Range Zoo and Victoria State Rose Garden: K Road, Werribee
☎ The Mansion: 131 963. Victoria State Rose Garden: 9742 6717. Open Range Zoo: 9731 9600; www.zoo.org.au
🕐 The Mansion: daily 10–5. Victoria State Rose Garden: daily 9–5. Open Range Zoo: daily 9–5
🍴 Kiosk
♿ Moderate

YARRA VALLEY

Northeast of Melbourne, the Yarra River is very different to how it is in the city.

In the pretty town of Eltham, don't miss the artists' colony at Montsalvat (▷ 98). At Yering, the Yarra Valley Dairy offers handmade cheeses and local cuisine. At the turn of the 20th century, 75 per cent of all Australian wines came from Victoria, and the Yarra Valley was one of the most productive wine regions in Australia. Today nearly 20 per cent of the nation's wines are produced in this region and its 35 vineyards welcome visitors and sell on their premises. Farther on is Healesville Sanctuary (▷ 99), with its native animal species in natural surroundings of bush-land and wetlands, and the nearby Galeena Beek Living Cultural Centre, where you can learn about Aboriginal culture and art. Many bus tours run to this district.

THE BASICS

Distance: 52km (32 miles) northeast of Melbourne
Journey Time: Allow a full day
ℹ Yarra Valley Visitor Information Centre
☎ 5962 2600
Australian Pacific Touring
☎ 9277 8555
Yarra Valley Dairy
✉ McMeikans Road, Yering
☎ 9739 0023
Yarra Winery Tours
☎ 9277 8555

Shopping

A1 MIDDLE EAST FOOD STORE

All the hard-to-get spices, oils and other exotic ingredients are here, plus breads and sweets.

🗷 Off map ✉ 43 Sydney Road, Brunswick ☎ 9386 04406 🚊 Tram 19

ARMADALE ANTIQUE CENTRE

Forty dealers sell a range of quality antiques and collectibles in this centre at the heart of popular Armadale high street's antique area.

🗷 Off map ✉ 1147 High Street, Armadale ☎ 9822 7788 ◑ Daily 9–5 🚊 Tram 6

CAMBERWELL SUNDAY MARKET

Several hundred stallholders converge here to sell assorted trash and treasures. A great place to observe the slow drift of suburban life.

🗷 Off map ✉ Station Street, Camberwell ◑ Sun 9–5 🚊 Tram 70

DE BORTOLI WINERY AND RESTAURANT

One of the best wineries and restaurants in the Yarra Valley, with fantastic views. Sample, then buy your wines, pick up some great cheeses and then dine on the excellent northern Italian food based on local produce. You need a car to get here.

🗷 Off map ✉ Pinnacle Lane, Dixons Creek ☎ 5965 2271

MATCHBOX

One of Melbourne's longest-established gift shops, specializing in design and new concepts and trends.

🗷 Off map ✉ 1050 High Street, Armadale ☎ 9824 6446 🚊 Tram 6

NATIONAL WOOL MUSEUM SHOP

An excellent range of wool products is for sale at Australia's only comprehensive wool museum, in a century-old wool store and featuring displays and hands-on exhibits highlighting all facets of this industry.

🗷 Off map ✉ 16 Moorabool Street, Geelong ☎ 5227 0701 ◑ Daily 9–5

PHILLIPPA'S BAKERY PROVISIONS

There's not much room to eat in here, but the huge selection of breads, cakes and other produce can yield a tasty takeaway lunch or picnic.

MEGA MALLS

A trip to any of Melbourne's major suburban shopping centres provides a chance to mingle with the locals in their own environment. You'll find cinemas and restaurants, as well as free entertainment. Try the Chadstone Shopping Centre (✉ 1341 Dandenong Road, Chadstone ◑ Mon–Wed, 9–5.30, Thu and Fri 9–9, Sat 9–5, Sun 10–5).

🗷 Off map ✉ 1030 High Street, Armadale ☎ 9576 2020 🚊 Tram 6

PIPEWORKS MARKET

The 500 shops, covered stalls and two food courts of this unique market complex sprawl over 8ha (20 acres). Live entertainment. You'll need a taxi to get here.

🗷 Off map ✉ 400 Mahoneys Road, Campbellfield ☎ 9357 1155 ◑ Sat–Sun 9–5

ST. KILDA

Melbourne's most vibrant suburb combines beachside frivolity with serious dining, great general shopping and a Sunday arts and crafts market (▷ 97 and below). Fitzroy Street and Acland Street are essential stops.

🗷 Off map ✉ Fitzroy and Acland streets, St. Kilda 🚊 Tram 96

ST. KILDA ESPLANADE MARKET

Original works made by stallholders at this popular Sunday arts and crafts market draw shoppers from far and wide.

🗷 Off map ✉ The Esplanade, St. Kilda ☎ 9534 0066 ◑ Sun 10–4 🚊 Tram 15, 16, 96

WILLIAMSTOWN

A waterfront village full of art, crafts, antique shops and coffee shops. People flock here on weekends.

🗷 Off map ✉ The Strand, Williamstown 🚉 Williamstown

Entertainment and Nightlife

ABSOLUTE OUTDOORS
Try your hand at abseiling, take a challenging mountain-bike ride and finish with a tranquil canoe tour in the spectacular Grampians National Park.
➕ Off map ✉ Shop 4, Stony Creek Stores, Halls Gap ☎ 5356 4556 ⏰ Daily tours

BALLOON SUNRISE
An adventurous way to view Melbourne is to take a hot-air balloon flight followed by a champagne breakfast.
➕ Off map ✉ 41 Dover Street, Richmond ☎ 9427 7596 ⏰ Daily at dawn

CLIFFHANGER CLIMBING GYM
Australia's tallest and most sophisticated indoor rock climbing facility; walls range from 6m (20ft) to 20m (66ft) tall.
➕ Off map ✉ Grieve Parade, Altona North ☎ 9369 6400 ⏰ Daily

DINNER PLAIN TRAIL RIDES
Based in the Dinner Plain Valley, near Mt Hotham, this company offers one day and multi-day riding trips into remote alpine areas.
➕ Off map ✉ PO Box 31, Dinner Plain ☎ 5159 6445 🚌 Rides on demand

DOG'S BAR
When you've finished with the serious Acland Street shopping, try this bar for great antipasto and canapés.
➕ Off map ✉ 54 Acland Street, St. Kilda ☎ 9525 3599 ⏰ Daily 🚋 Tram 16

THE ESPLANADE
On weekends, local music lovers pack this St. Kilda institution, a legend among those who love pub music. You can have a meal in the restaurant at the back or watch the sunset.
➕ Off map ✉ Upper Esplanade, St. Kilda ☎ 9534 0211 ⏰ Daily 🚋 Tram 16

FLEMINGTON RACECOURSE
This famous racecourse hosts the annual Melbourne Cup and has a regular programme of race days year-round.
➕ Off map ✉ Smithfield Road, Flemington ☎ 9371 7171 🚋 Tram 57

WATER SPORTS
Melbourne's location on Port Phillip Bay provides great opportunities for water sports. You can surf at Mornington Peninsula and near Flinders, windsurf from Sandringham (☎ 9598 2867), go diving in the bay (☎ 9459 4111), or sail with the Melbourne Sailing School (☎ 9589 1433). Swim at the bayside beaches close to Melbourne, between Port Melbourne and St. Kilda, and from St. Kilda to Portsea, and in the many public pools around the city and in the suburbs.

MERIDIAN KAYAK ADVENTURES
Explore the sea at close quarters along Victoria's spectacular coast: Wilsons Promontory, Cape Otway, the Twelve Apostles etc...
➕ Off map ✉ 12 Clonard Avenue, Elsternwick ☎ 1300 656 433 ⏰ Tours on demand

MOONRAKER DOLPHIN SWIMS
On boat tours in pristine Port Phillip Bay, you may choose to swim with the wild dolphins or simply sightsee in comfort.
➕ Off map ✉ St Aubins Way, Sorrento ☎ 5984 4211 ⏰ Tours on demand

THE PRINCE BAND ROOM
A hot-spot venue for top musicians, with quality club gear and lighting.
➕ Off map ✉ 29 Fitzroy Street, St. Kilda ☎ 9536 1168 ⏰ Daily, usually from 8pm 🚋 Tram 96

RIVIERA NAUTIC
Sail to a variety of destinations on a choice of yachts; equipment provided.
➕ Off map ✉ Chinamans Creek, Metung ☎ 5156 2243 ⏰ On demand

ST. KILDA SEA BATHS
Near St. Kilda pier, the complex houses a 25m public pool, gym facilities and spa, plus restaurants.
➕ Off map ✉ 10–18 Jacka Boulevard, St. Kilda ☎ 9525 4888 ⏰ Mon–Thu 5.30am–10pm, Fri 5.30am–9pm, Sat–Sun 8–8 🚋 Tram 96

Restaurants

PRICES

Prices are approximate, based on a 3-course meal for one person.

$	A$10–A$20
$$	A$21–A$44
$$$	A$45–A$90

CIRCA ($$$)

This restaurant has achieved near perfection with its attention to detail, discreet service, elegant setting and innovative modern British food. It's also pricey.

Off map ⊠ 2 Acland Street, St. Kilda ☎ 9534 5033 ⏺ Lunch and dinner daily 🚋 Tram 16

DONOVANS ($$–$$$)

This St. Kilda favourite, in a good beachside location, serves Mediterranean dishes with a modern twist.

Off map ⊠ 40 Jacka Boulevard, St. Kilda ☎ 9534 8221 ⏺ Lunch Mon–Fri, dinner daily 🚋 Tram 16

HARRY'S ($$)

Close to the water at Queenscliff, with mostly outdoor seating. Although you can order other dishes besides seafood, don't miss the mussels in white wine. Car needed.

Off map ⊠ Princes Park, Queenscliff ☎ 5258 3750 ⏺ Lunch Fri–Sun, dinner Thu–Sun

THE HEALESVILLE HOTEL ($$)

Country pub with a contemporary menu and interesting wine list.

Off map ⊠ 256 Maroondah Highway, Healesville ☎ 5962 4002 ⏺ Lunch and dinner daily

KENLOCK LICENSED RESTAURANT ($$)

Fine international dining and an excellent wine cellar feature at this country manor-house restaurant.

Off map ⊠ Mt Dandenong Tourist Road, Olinda ☎ 9751 1008 ⏺ Lunch Wed–Sun., dinner Fri–Sat

OZONE HOTEL ($$)

Contemporary fare is served at this famous old hotel. You will also find an excellent wine list.

Off map ⊠ 42 Gellibrand Street, Queenscliff ☎ 9739 0023 ⏺ Lunch and dinner daily

AUSTRALIAN SEAFOOD

It is not surprising that seafood is so popular in this bayside city. Local specialties include Melbourne rock oysters, kingfish, enormous prawns, Tasmanian scallops, smoked salmon and South Australian tuna. Northern fish such as the delicious barramundi grace menus all over town. Appropriately, many seafood restaurants have waterfront locations, where you can buy excellent fish and chips to go—St. Kilda, Brighton and Williamstown are particularly good spots for alfresco eating.

PEPPERS DELGANY ($$$)

French, Mediterranean and Asian flavours mingle at this magnificent old place, with consistently good food.

Off map ⊠ Point Nepean Road, Portsea ☎ 5984 4000 ⏺ Breakfast, lunch and dinner daily

SAILS ON THE BAY ($$–$$$)

Fresh seafood is the specialty of this waterfront restaurant, with fine views day and night.

Off map ⊠ 15 Elwood Foreshore, Elwood ☎ 9525 6933 ⏺ Lunch and dinner daily 🚋 Tram 16

SAPORE ($$–$$$)

This trendy restaurant serves modern Italian food in a bold, streamlined setting. Classic desserts and good value.

Off map ⊠ 3 Fitzroy Street, St. Kilda ☎ 9534 9666 ⏺ Lunch Tue–Sun, dinner daily 🚋 Tram 16

WILD OAK CAFÉ ($$)

This rustic café presents a mixed menu that includes heartier fare in winter.

Off map ⊠ 232 Ridge Road, Mt Dandenong ☎ 9751 2033 ⏺ Lunch and dinner daily

YARRA VALLEY DAIRY ($$)

In this dairy barn, fitted out as a café, you can sample fine cheeses.

Off map ⊠ McMeikan's Road, Yering ☎ 5258 1011 ⏺ Lunch and dinner daily

Melbourne offers every category of accommodation—from budget backpacker hostels to international-standard deluxe hotels where you are liable to pay A$300 or more per night.

Where to Stay

Introduction

Take your pick from a range of areas to stay, in all types of accommodation. You may prefer the quieter suburbs to the buzz of central Melbourne.

A Wide Choice

Melbourne has plenty of accommodation options. At the upper end there's the luxurious Westin (▷ 112) and the Stamford Plaza (▷ 112), and the less expensive, but classy, boutique Prince (▷ 111) at St. Kilda. At the lower end is the ever popular Melbourne Metro YHA. There are also many economical, self-catering apartments and reasonably priced guesthouses, and hostels are plentiful. Bed-and-breakfasts are numerous, especially in outer suburbs and rural areas close to the city.

Where to Stay

Melbourne's major hotel areas are around the city centre, East Melbourne, North Melbourne and Southbank. Most hotels have in-room inter-net connections or wireless areas for laptops, and all backpacker hostels have computers for pay-as-you-go net surfing and email checking.

Get a Bargain

It's worth looking on the internet for special deals, for both advance bookings and last-minute rate reductions. But be aware that there are popular times of the year, such as around Melbourne Cup time (early November) and the Grand Prix (mid-March), when hotels are fully booked, so forward booking is essential.

STAY AT THE AIRPORT

Although Melbourne's CBD is only 22km (14 miles) from the international airport, there are times when a stay at an airport hotel is necessary. Fortunately there are three good options, one in each of the price ranges, budget, mid-range and luxury. Hotel Formule 1 Melbourne Airport (☎ 8336-1811) is a good budget option; Melbourne Airport Motel offers mid-range value (☎ 1800 337 046); Hilton Melbourne Airport (☎ 8336 2000) is the top-end choice.

Budget Hotels

PRICES

Expect to pay under A$100 for a double room per night in a budget hotel.

ASTORIA CITY TRAVEL INN

Not far from the main railway station, this motel is a safe choice, with its own restaurant and good clean rooms.

🏠 B5 ✉ 288 Spencer Street ☎ 9670 680;, fax 9670 3034 🚇 Spencer Street

CITY CENTRE BUDGET HOTEL

www.citycentrebudgethotel.com.au

One of the best hotels in this price range; wireless internet, shared bathrooms and rooftop deck.

🏠 G5 ✉ 22–30 Little Collins Street ☎ 9654 540;, fax 9650 7256 🚋 City Circle Tram

CLAREMONT GUESTHOUSE

www.hotelclaremont.com

Convenient guesthouse with communal facilities and bright rooms.

🏠 Off map ✉ 189 Toorak Road, South Yarra ☎ 9826 8000; fax 9827 8652 🚋 Tram 8

GEORGIAN COURT BED-AND-BREAKFAST

www.georgiancourt.com.au

An elegant bed-and-breakfast with a variety of rooms.

🏠 Off map ✉ 21–23 George Street, East Melbourne ☎ 9419 6353; fax 9416 0895 🚋 Tram 48, 75

GLOBAL BACKPACKERS

Just opposite the Queen Victoria Market, this top section of an old pub has good facilities and an indoor rock-climbing wall.

🏠 C3 ✉ 238 Victoria Street ☎ 9328 3728; fax 9329 8966 🚋 City Circle Tram

JASPER HOTEL

www.jasperhotel.com.au

This hotel offers a good range of reasonably priced accommodation, plus a fitness centre, an indoor pool and café.

🏠 D4 ✉ 489 Elizabeth Street ☎ 8327 2778; fax 9329 1469 🚋 City Circle Tram

MELBOURNE METRO YHA

www.yha.com.au

BACKPACKING

Melbourne has many backpacker lodges with accommodation varing from private rooms to dormitories. Prices start at A$10 per night and most places offer reduced rates for long stays. The best backpacker areas are in the city, North Melbourne and the beach suburb of St. Kilda. Another inexpensive accommodation option is staying at the Australian version of the local pub, but often referred to as a hotel. More details can be obtainined from the Victorian Tourism Information Service (☎ 132 842).

Over 300 rooms, with fine facilities, a travel agency and good travel information. This is near Queen Victoria Market and not far from the city centre.

🏠 C3 ✉ 78 Howard Street, North Melbourne ☎ 9329 8599; fax 9326 8427 🚋 Tram 57

THE NUNNERY

www.nunnery.com.au

Clean, centrally-heated rooms, comfortable communal facilities, and a great atmosphere ensure that this place remains popular with budget travellers.

🏠 Off map ✉ 116 Nicholson Street, Fitzroy ☎ 9419 8637; fax 9417 7736 🚋 Tram 96

ST. KILDA COFFEE PALACE

www.coffeepalace.backpackers.com.au

One of the city's most popular backpackers' hostels, close to the action in St Kilda. Has a rooftop garden, friendly staff and an excellent bulletin board where you can get great travel information.

🏠 Off map ✉ 24 Grey Street, St. Kilda ☎ 9534 5283; fax 9534 2005 🚋 Tram 16, 96

TOAD HALL

www.toadhall.hotel.com.au

There is a choice of dorm or private rooms at this popular and conveniently located hostel.

🏠 D4 ✉ 441 Elizabeth Street ☎ 9600 9010; fax 9600 9013 🚋 City Circle Tram

Mid-Range Hotels

PRICES

Expect to pay between A$100 and A$195 per night for a double room in a mid-range hotel.

ALL SEASONS KINGSGATE HOTEL

www.accorhotels.com.au
Within walking distance of many attractions, this friendly hotel has 101 spacious rooms, with all the usual amenities, plus an on-site restaurant and bar.

C6 ⊠ 131 King Street
☎ 9629 4171; fax 9629 7110
🚊 Tram 86, 96

ATLANTIS HOTEL

www.atlantishotel.com.au
Situated near most major attractions, theatres and department stores, this stylish hotel has suites with great views over the city and Victoria Harbour.

B5 ⊠ 300 Spencer Street
☎ 9600 2900; fax 9600 2700
🚊 Tram 86

BATMAN'S ON COLLINS

www.batmanshill.com.au
This hotel is just a few minutes' stroll from the Crown Entertainment Complex, the Yarra River, the new Colonial Stadium and Spencer Street Station.

C7 ⊠ 66 Spencer Street
☎ 9614 6344; fax 9614 1189
🚊 Spencer Street

HOTEL CAUSEWAY

www.causeway.com.au
Surrounded by boutiques and eateries, this conveniently located hotel offers non-smoking and disabled rooms, business and fitness centres, and a delicious buffet breakfast.

E6 ⊠ 275 Little Collins Street ☎ 9660 8888; fax 9660 8877 🚊 Any Swanston Street tram

DOWNTOWNER ON LYGON

www.downtowner.com.au
Within easy walking distance of the city, the Queen Victoria Market and the varied restaurants of Lygon Street, this friendly hotel is of a very high standard.

E3 ⊠ 66 Lygon Street
☎ 9663 5555; fax 9662 3308
🚊 City Circle Tram

ENTERPRISE HOTEL

www.hotelenterprise.com.au
Comfortable and affordable, this hotel has two types of accommodation

COUNTRY STYLE

Be sure to experience the green splendour of the Dandenong Ranges, an hour east of the city centre. One of the best places to stay here is Arcadia Cottages (⊠ 188 Falls Road, Olinda ☎ 9751 1017). These superbly furnished and individually crafted cottages are set in an attractive garden and include hot tubs and cozy wood-fired heaters. Be sure to reserve ahead because they are popular.

suitable for both business and budget travellers and is close to popular attractions and transportation terminals.

C7 ⊠ 44 Spencer Street
☎ 9629 6991; fax 9614 7963
🚊 Any Flinders Street tram

HOTEL GRAND CHANCELLOR

www.ghihotels.com.au
In the heart of the city, with Chinatown and the theatre district on its doorstep, this excellent and comfortable hotel has the feel of many places with much higher rates.

F5 ⊠ 131 Lonsdale Street
☎ 9656 4000; fax 9662 3479
🚊 City Circle Tram

MAGNOLIA COURT BOUTIQUE HOTEL

www.magnolia-court.com.au
A family-run boutique hotel with its own breakfast café. Rooms range from a luxury self-contained apartment to compact units.

J5 ⊠ 101 Powlett Street, East Melbourne ☎ 9419 4222; fax 9416 0841 🚊 Tram 48, 75 from Flinders Street

MARQUE HOTEL

www.marquehotels.com
With 80 deluxe boutique rooms, plus a restaurant and bar, Marque is located in the café precinct of the beachside suburb of St. Kilda and only 10 minutes from the city by tram.

Off map ⊠ 35–37 Fitzroy Street, St. Kilda ☎ 8530 8888; fax 8530 8800
🚊 Tram 16

MECURE WELCOME HOTEL

www.mecurewelcome.com.au
In a handy location, right
in the centre of the city,
close to the major department stores and the
Central Business District,
this popular hotel is very
convenient and has great
facilities, all at a reasonable price.

⊞ E5 ⊠ 265 Little Bourke
Street ☎ 9639 0555; fax
9650 3920 🚋 City Circle
Tram

MEDINA EXECUTIVE NORTHBANK

www.medina.com.au
Located right at the
heart of Melbourne's
attractions; convenient
for the Royal Botanical
Gardens, Rod Laver Arena
and the Yarra River. There
are well-maintained
kitchens, swimming pool,
sauna, spa and massage
service. No restaurant, but
there are plenty of top
eateries nearby.

⊞ G6 ⊠ 88 Flinders Street
☎ 9246 0000; fax 9246 0199
🚋 Trams 48, 70, 75

OAKS ON COLLINS

www.theoaksgroup.com.au
This comfortable
apartment hotel is
conveniently situated in
the CBD near Southgate
and the Crown Casino.
It has New York-style
studio apartments, a
restaurant and lounge
bar, 10m (33ft) lap pool,
gym and sauna.

⊞ E6 ⊠ 480 Collins Street
☎ 8610 6444; fax 8610 6488
🚋 Trams 109, 112

PARKVIEW ST. KILDA ROAD HOTEL

www.viewhotels.com.au
Located not far from the
city, Parkview has well
appointed rooms, a
restaurant and bar, roof-
top spa and sauna, and
is close to the shopping
and attractions in
St. Kilda, Southbank and
the CBD.

⊞ Off map ⊠ 562 St. Kilda
Road ☎ 9529 888; fax 9525
1242 🚋 Tram 3, 5, 6, 64,
67, 72

THE PRINCE

www.theprince.com.au
Nothing quite matches a
stay at this particularly
stylish and elegant bou-
tique hotel, home of one
of the city's top restau-
rants, Circa (▷ 106).

⊞ Off map ⊠ 2 Acland
Street, St. Kilda ☎ 9536 1111;
fax 9536 1100 🚋 Tram 16

APARTMENTS

Renting quarters in one of
Melbourne's apartment-style
hotels generally falls into the
moderate price range. Many
of these apartments, with full
maid service, are large
enough for families or small
groups. They have from one
to three bedrooms, with
separate dining areas and
kitchens or kitchenettes, so
you can cook your own
meals if it suits you. One of
the best of these is The
Saville on Russell (⊠ 222
Russell Street ☎ 9915 2500)
in the CBD.

RADISSON ON FLAGSTAFF GARDENS

www.radisson.com
The reliable Radisson is
conveniently located in
the heart of the city,
opposite historic Flagstaff
Gardens, this 184-room
hotel has a health and
fitness centre, a business
centre, non-smoking
floors and convenient
valet parking.

⊞ C5 ⊠ 380 William Street
☎ 9322 8000; fax 9322 8888
🚋 City Circle Tram

HOTEL SOPHIA

www.hotelsophia.com.au
On the corner of King
and Little Lonsdale
streets, this property has
non-smoking rooms,
wireless internet connec-
tion to all rooms, a
restaurant and bar, and
facilities and services for
the disabled traveller.

⊞ C5 ⊠ 277–287 King
Street ☎ 9670 1342; fax
9602 1018 🚋 Trams 86, 96

TRAVELODGE HOTEL SOUTHBANK

www.travelodge.com.au
Easy walking distance to
the aquarium, art gal-
leries, the Crown Casino,
Royal Botanic Gardens
and the Melbourne
Exhibition Centre. Air-
conditioned rooms, all
amenities, and a local
restaurant will deliver
right to your room.

⊞ E7 ⊠ 9 Riverside Quay,
Southbank, (a short walk
across the bridge from
Flinders Street Station)
☎ 8696 9600; fax 9690 1160
🚋 Flinders Street

Luxury Hotels

PRICES

Expect to pay over A$195 per night for a double room at a luxury hotel.

THE COMO

www.mirvachotels.com.au
This top hotel offers studios and suites, great food, a gymnasium, sauna and pool. It's near some of Melbourne's most popular shops and restaurants.

➕ Off map ✉ 630 Chapel Street, South Yarra ☎ 9824 0400; fax 9824 1263 🚊 Tram 78, 79

CROWN PROMENADE

www.crownpromenade.com.au
The ultimate in luxury, this hotel, with the casino, world-class health centre, classy shopping centres and stylish waterfront restaurants at its doorstep. Treat youself to something special.

➕ E7 ✉ Southbank ☎ 9292 6688; fax 9292 6299 🚉 Flinders Street 🚊 Tram 10, 12, 96, 109

GRAND HYATT MELBOURNE

www.melbourne.grand.hyatt.com
One of Melbourne's best hotels, the Grand Hyatt has very good restaurants, a health and fitness centre, first-class business facilities and exclusive boutiques.

➕ F6 ✉ 123 Collins Street ☎ 9657 1234; fax 9650 3491 🚊 City Circle Tram

LANGHAM HOTEL

www.langhamhotels.com.au
Close to the Arts Centre action and the Crown Entertainment Complex, this top hotel has a business centre, a health club and a heated pool.

➕ E7 ✉ 1 Southgate Avenue (short walk from city centre) ☎ 8696 8888; fax 9690 5889

PARK HYATT MELBOURNE

www.melbourne.park.hyatt.com
This luxury hotel provides a warm, distinctive ambience and good service.

➕ Off map ✉ 1 Parliament Place ☎ 9224 1234; fax 9224 1200 🚊 City Circle Tram

RIALTO HOTEL ON COLLINS

www.rialtohotel.com.au
Stylish luxury hotel in a

DAY SPAS

Many of Melbourne's hotels have put aside areas to cater for this popular form of indulgence, where you can renew the body, mind and soul and leave revitalized and refreshed. Treatments include facials, several different types of massage, including remedial and deep tissue, and practitioners in naturopathy, acupuncture and aromatherapy may be on hand. Good choices include the Park Club Health and Day Spa at the Park Hyatt (▷ this page) and Aurora Spa Retreat at The Prince hotel (▷ 111).

heritage-listed building, with top service, a great location next to the Rialto Towers, bars, a brasserie and a heated rooftop pool and sauna.

➕ D7 ✉ 495 Collins Street ☎ 9620 9111; fax 9614 1219 🚊 City Circle Tram

STAMFORD PLAZA

www.stamford.com.au
This all-suite hotel is within walking distance of theatres, cinemas and the exclusive end of Collins Street.

➕ F5 ✉ 111 Little Collins Street ☎ 9659 1000; fax 9659 0999 🚊 City Circle Tram

WESTIN

www.westin.com.au
Centrally located within the business and entertainment district, this five-star hotel has spacious rooms and suites, superb amenities, and Allegro, one of the city's best restaurants.

➕ F6 ✉ 205 Collins Street ☎ 9635 2222; fax 9635 2333 🚊 City Circle Tram

WINDSOR HOTEL

www.windsor.com.au
One of the world's finest hotels and certainly Australia's grandest and most steeped in history, this Oberoi chain hotel offers fine service and a sense of style. Even if you don't stay here, check it out.

➕ G5 ✉ 111 Spring Street ☎ 9633 6002; fax 9633 6001 🚊 City Circle Tram

The more you plan your trip, the more you'll get out of your time in Melbourne, which has so much to offer. These pages of travel advice and facts will give you insider knowledge of the city.

Need to Know

Planning Ahead

When to Go

Summer is the best time to visit Melbourne, when festivals and celebrations are happening all over the city, plus it's perfect weather for a trip to the beach or walks in Melbourne's many beautiful parks and gardens. Be sure to pre-book accommodation in busy periods.

TIME

Daylight Saving operates from the last Sunday in October to the last Sunday in March (11 hours ahead of GMT).

AVERAGE DAILY MAXIMUM TEMPERATURES

JAN	FEB	MAR	APR	MAY	JUN	JUL	AUG	SEP	OCT	NOV	DEC
79°F	77°F	75°F	68°F	63°F	57°F	55°F	59°F	63°F	68°F	72°F	75°F
26°C	25°C	24°C	20°C	17°C	14°C	13°C	15°C	17°C	20°C	22°C	24°C

Melbourne's weather changes frequently ('four seasons in a day')–always carry an umbrella, even if it doesn't look like rain. The city enjoys a generally temperate climate.

Spring (September–November) is cool to mild, with average highs of 20°C and average lows of 10°C, perfect for being out and about.

Summer (December–February) can be warm to hot, and many locals head for the beaches.

Autumn (March–May) is mild–good weather for parks and gardens.

Winter (June–August) can be wet and cool, when Melburnians retreat to the city's cosy cafés, bars and shopping venues.

WHAT'S ON

January *Cricket matches*: Take place day and night at the famous Melbourne Cricket Ground.
Australian Open Tennis: The classic tournament is at Melbourne Park.

March *Qantas Australian Grand Prix*: Albert Park.
The Moomba Festival: A Melbourne cultural institution that includes parades and exhibitions.

April *Melbourne Food and Wine Festival*: The place to sample Australia's best food and wines.
Melbourne International

Flower and Garden Show: Indoor exhibition of plants and garden products.
Melbourne International Comedy Festival: One of the largest comedy festivals in the world.
Rip Curl Pro and Sun Smart Classic: Australia's most prestigious surfing event is held at Torquay.

June *Melbourne International Film Festival*: A showcase for top local and international movies.

August *Australian Antiques and Fine Art Fair*: The state's premier antiques fair.

September *Australian Rules Grand Final*: The city comes to a halt as the top teams compete.
Royal Melbourne Show: Eleven days of animals, events, food, art and crafts.

October/November *Melbourne Cup and the Spring Racing Carnival*: The Melbourne Cup is the highlight of this series of prestigious races.
Melbourne Festival: Art exhibitions, concerts, plays and dance performance.

December *New Year's Eve*: Fireworks and partying.

Melbourne Online

Most hotels in Melbourne will have internet access in the rooms, an area with wireless connections for laptops or an online computer set up in the lobby.

www.melbourne.vic.gov.au

Melbourne's official website for tourists has up-to-date, comprehensive information on city attractions, events, guided tours, shopping, accommodation, eating out and lots more.

www.visitmelbourne.com

Melbourne's best travel and accommodation website, with special interest categories such as families, students, gay and lesbian, disabled travellers, and backpackers.

www.hotelclub.com

An Australian and worldwide hotel booking service offering special deals on accommodation, travel insurance, car rental, tours and airline bookings. Written in 10 languages.

www.bom.gov.au

The national bureau of meteorology, with comprehensive weather information and forecasts—very handy, since Melbourne weather is very changeable.

www.theage.com.au

The Age is Melbourne's major daily newspaper, with excellent coverage of the latest local, national and world news stories, as well as sections on breaking news and business, travel, technology and entertainment.

www.smartraveller.com.au

This is the Australian Government travel advisory service. As well as travel alerts, the site allows you to register your particulars so that you can be contacted in an emergency. It links to sites providing a range of information, including travel insurance, health insurance and cheap airline flights.

PRIME TRAVEL SITES

www.metlinkmelbourne. com.au
For train, tram and bus information, timetables, maps of stations and stops, fares, tickets, and a journey planner.

www.melbourneairport. com.au
Information on arrival and departure times, shopping and eating, Duty Free shops, facilities and services, and an airport map.

www.fodors.com
A complete travel-planning site. You can research prices and weather; reserve air tickets, cars and rooms; pose questions (and get answers) to fellow visitors; and find links to other sites.

INTERNET CAFÉS

Global Gossip
➕ C5 ✉ 440 Elizabeth Street ☎ 9663 0511
🕐 Daily 9am–11pm
💷 $3 per half hour

Traveller Contact Point
➕ G5 ✉ 29–31 Somerset Place (off Little Bourke Street) ☎ 9642 2911
🕐 Daily 10am–11pm
💷 $3 per half hour

Getting There

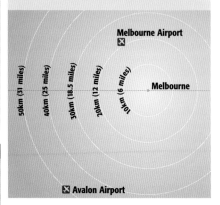

WHAT TO PACK

● In summer (December–February) the temperature averages 25°C (77°F). Take cotton clothing, a broad-brimmed hat, sunglasses and other summer-weight items, plus an umbrella.

● In winter (June–August) take a raincoat and/or medium-weight coat, plus clothing suitable for an average 13°C (55°F).

BEFORE YOU GO

● All visitors require a valid passport and an ETA (Electronic Travel Authority). It is fully electronic and is available through travel agents.

● A Tourist ETA is valid for one year (or until the expiry date of your passport, if less), allows for multiple entry and will allow you to stay for a total of three months. Australia does not allow entry if your passport expires within six months of your entry date.

● Vaccination certificates are not normally required, unless you have travelled to an infected country within the previous 14 days.

● Australian Tourist Commission office: Gemini House, Putney Hill, London SW15 ☎ Administration only: 020 8780 2229. Brochure line: 0870 556 1434.

AIRPORTS

Melbourne Airport is 22km (14 miles) northwest of Melbourne's Central Business District (CBD). Avalon Airport is 50km (31 miles) southwest of central Melbourne.

Melbourne Airport ⊠

Melbourne

50km (31 miles) · 40km (25 miles) · 30km (18.5 miles) · 20km (12 miles) · 10km (6 miles)

⊠ **Avalon Airport**

ARRIVING BY AIR

Melbourne Airport (www.melbourneairport.com.au) at Tullamarine, to the north of the city, is the main port of entry for overseas visitors on direct flights. The airport also handles the majority of domestic passenger arrivals. There are taxis and inexpensive bus services (including Skybus ☎ 9600 1711; www.skybus.com.au) travel into the city, as well as car rental outlets. A second airport, south-west of the city, Avalon Airport, serves domestic carrier JetStar's flights, and the Sunbus (☎ 9689 6888) service meets all flights that arrive there.

ARRIVING BY SEA

Not the most common means by which to arrive in Melbourne, but the city is an increasingly popular port for cruise liners. Melbourne's Station Pier, 4km (2.5 miles) from the city, serves cruise ships as well as being the dock of the *Spirit of Tasmania* (☎ 1800 634 906; www.spiritoftasmania.com.au), the car and passenger ferry service between Melbourne and Devonport in Tasmania. A tram runs to and

SPIRIT OF TASMANIA

from the pier to Collins Street in the city approximately every 15 minutes.

ARRIVING BY BUS

Bus travel is often more expensive than flying, but buses are nevertheless one of the best ways to see more of Australia and Victoria on your way to Melbourne. Country and interstate buses pick up and depart from the Melbourne Transit Centre at 58 Franklin Street, near the top of Swanston Street. Day and overnight buses arrive each day from Adelaide and Sydney and usually take between 11 and 12 hours. The main interstate carrier is Greyhound Australia (☎ 4690 9950; www.greyhound.com.au).

ARRIVING BY TRAIN

Country and interstate trains (☎ 9697 2076; www.vline.com.au) travel to and around Victoria and offer a comfortable, if slower, way to see the state and other parts of Australia. Vline trains arrive at Southern Cross Station, part of the metropolitan train system's underground City Loop service. Countrylink XPT train services (☎ 13 22 42; www.countrylink.info) from Sydney to Melbourne takes around 10–11 hours.

ARRIVING BY CAR

Car rental is inexpensive in Australia and is a popular way for families to save money on inter-capital travel. The main highways between cities are excellent. Melbourne and larger regional centres have several car rental firms, offering a variety of vehicles and deals. You must be at least 25 years old, and you can pay additional fees to have the insurance excess waived. The main rental companies are Avis, Budget, Europcar, Hertz, National and Thrifty. Remember there are great distances involved in driving between Australian state capitals and to the many isolated attractions, so good planning is essential for a successful driving holiday. And driving in outback locations requires extra precautions and good driving skills. Check www.aaa.asn.au for more details.

CUSTOMS REGULATIONS

● Visitors aged 18 or over may bring in 250 cigarettes or 250g of tobacco or cigars; 1,125ml of alcoholic spirits; plus other dutiable goods to the value of A$400 per person.
● There is no limit on money imported for personal use, although amounts in excess of A$5,000 or its equivalent must be declared on arrival.
● The smuggling of all drugs is treated harshly in Australia, and the importing of firearms and items such as ivory or other products from endangered species is illegal or restricted.

EMERGENCY TELEPHONE NUMBERS

Police, Ambulance and Fire
☎ 000 (24 hours)
Calls are free.

Consulates
Canada: ☎ 9563 9674
France: ☎ 9602 5024
Germany: ☎ 9864 6888
UK: ☎ 9652 1670
US: ☎ 9526 5900

POLICE

The non-emergency police number is ☎ 9247 6666. Melbourne's police wear blue uniforms and a peaked cap. They are generally helpful and polite.

Getting Around

DISCOUNT AND MAPS

● Metcard tickets allow for travel on trams, trains and buses within the zones marked on the ticket. Three fare zones apply: Zone 1 covers most of the CBD area and inner suburbs. Zones 2 and 3 extend to the outer fringes of the Melbourne area. Check out: ☎ 13 1638; www.metlinkmelbourne. com.au

● A two-hour ticket (A$3.30 and up) allows unlimited travel for two hours, daily tickets (A$6.30 and up) for the whole day. Short-trip tickets, two-hour tickets and 60 Plus tickets for senior citizens, a seniors daily ticket, may be purchased on board trams and buses. Sunday Saver tickets cost A$2.50. All Metcard tickets can be bought at rail stations from Customer Service Centres and vending machines, at retail outlets displaying the Metcard sign or flag, and at the City Met Shop at 103 Elizabeth Street.

● Get free public transport maps from stations and the Met Shop in Elizabeth Street.

FEMALE TRAVELLERS

Melbourne is generally a safe place for women travellers. However, walking alone in parks or on beaches at night, and travelling alone on out-of-city-centre trains at night, is not recommended.

Melbourne's excellent public transportation system is centred around its tram and light rail system.

TRAMS AND LIGHT RAIL

Principal services operate from Swanston and Elizabeth streets (north and south); Flinders, Collins and Bourke streets and Batman Avenue (east and west). Trams operate between 5am and midnight Mon–Sat, and 7am and 11pm Sun.

The distinctive burgundy and gold free City Circle Trams run in both directions around the entire city centre, at 12-minute intervals, between 10am and 6pm daily.

Other methods of transport and taxis for hire in the city are as follows:

AIRPORT BUS

Skybus runs to Melbourne Airport, around the clock, daily. Drop-offs and pick-ups are available at hotels and at Southern Cross Bus Station. Cost is A$15 for adults and A$5 for children ☎ 9600 1711.

BUSES

Melbourne's buses vary in colour, depending on the company. Skybus (☎ 9600 1722; www.skybus.com.au) runs between Melbourne Airport and the city terminus. Privately run Explorer buses take passengers around the main sights.

There are no specific bus terminals for suburban buses. Catch them at designated stops. Ordinary tickets are available on board. Buy special passes (▷ see panel) at kiosks and news-agencies as well as from the driver. Privately run Nightrider Buses can take you home safely between 12.30am and 4.30am on Saturday or Sunday mornings for A$320. They head for various suburban destinations and run at hourly intervals, picking up at designated stops, including those close to the major nightlife venues.

CAR HIRE

Hiring a car may be necessary for some of the out-of-town trips within this book. You must be over 25. Compulsory third-party insurance is included in rental prices, which are on average A$70–A$90 per day. Overseas visitors require an international driving licence.

Major Melbourne car rental companies are: Avis ☎ 136 333; Budget ☎ 132 727 and Hertz ☎ 133 039.

Full details of Australia's road rules are available from the Australian Automobile Association in Canberra ☎ (02) 6247 7311; www.aaa.asn.au

FERRIES

Ferries run from Southgate and from World Trade Centre wharves. These are primarily for tours but a ferry runs to Williamstown, from Southbank and St. Kilda, as public transport. Buy tickets directly from the operators.

TAXIS

Taxis are meter-operated, yellow and conspicuously marked with a 'Taxi' sign on top of the vehicle. The basic charge is around A$3.10 (plus a booking fee of A$1.30) and the remainder of the fare is calculated based on time and distance (A$1.15 per kilometre). A small additional booking fee is charged for taxis ordered by phone. A surcharge of A$2 applies after midnight.

Main operators include Arrow ☎ 132 211; 13 Cabs ☎ 132 227; Embassy ☎ 131 755; and Silver Top ☎ 131 008. Ask for a taxi that can take a wheelchair if you need one.

TRAINS

Melbourne's inner-city rail lines include the City Loop (Parliament, Melbourne Central, Flagstaff Gardens, Spencer Street and Flinders Street Station).

Flinders Street Station is the main suburban rail terminus. Buy tickets from booths or machines, and enter platforms via the automatic barriers. Trains operate 5am–midnight Mon–Sat, 7am–11pm Sun.

ETIQUETTE

● Smoking is prohibited on public transport (including all internal flights and inside airport terminals), in cinemas, theatres, shops and shopping centres. Some restaurants provide smoking areas.

● Dress is generally smart-casual. Casual clothing for women and shorts for men are usual in summer, even in the city centre.

● Tipping is expected only in restaurants. Service charges are not normally added to bills, so a 10 per cent tip is the norm. Tipping taxi drivers and hotel staff is optional.

STUDENT TRAVELLERS

● International Student Identity Cards are not usually recognized by cinemas, theatres or public transport authorities, but you may be able to get concessions on bus travel.

● There are many backpackers' lodges, YHA establishments and hostels in Melbourne (all busy in summer). YHA cardholders may obtain discounts.

TRAVEL INSURANCE

Ensure you have appropriate cover before departure.

Essential Facts

OPENING HOURS

● Shops: in the city centre generally Mon–Thu 10–6; Fri 10–9; Sat–Sun 10–6. Suburban hours vary; corner shops often open daily 8–8 or later.

● Banks: Mon–Thu 9.30–4; Fri 9.30–5. City head-office banks open Mon–Fri 8.15–5.

● Museums and galleries: generally daily 10–5. Some close on one day of the week and hours may vary from day to day.

● Offices: Mon–Fri 9–5 (5.30 in some cases).

● Restaurants: some close on Sun or Mon.

MONEY

The Australian unit of currency is the Australian dollar (A$), comprising 100 cents. Banknotes come in A$100, A$50, A$20, A$10 and A$5 denominations. Coins come in 5¢, 10¢, 20¢ and 50¢ (silver), and A$1 and A$2 (gold coloured).

5 dollars

10 dollars

50 dollars

100 dollars

ELECTRICITY

● The electricity supply in Australia is 230–250 volts AC. Three-flat-pin plugs are the standard but are not the same as in the UK and adaptors are needed.

● Hotels provide standard 110-volt and 240-volt shaver sockets.

GOODS & SERVICES TAX (GST)

A 10 per cent GST applies to all goods and services. The charge is sometimes added to bills, but is often included in listed prices.

INTERNATIONAL NEWSAGENTS

UK and US newspapers, as well as many foreign-language papers, are available from larger newsagents around the city centre, including Mitty's News Agency, 53 Bourke Street.

NATIONAL, STATE AND SCHOOL HOLIDAYS

● 1 January: New Year's Day
● 26 January: Australia Day
● 2nd Monday in March: Labour Day (Victorian state holiday)
● Good Friday
● Easter Monday
● 25 April: Anzac Day
● 2nd Monday in June: Queen's Birthday
● 1st Tuesday in November: Melbourne Cup
● 25 December: Christmas Day
● 26 December: Christmas holiday
● School summer holidays are mid-December to late January—transport, accommodation and tourist facilities are heavily booked at this time.

NEWSPAPERS

● The main national daily newspaper is *The Australian*; read *The Australian Financial Review* for business news.

● The city's daily newspapers are *The Age*, giving a reasonable coverage of international news, and *The Herald Sun*, a tabloid-style paper published in several editions throughout the day.

MAGAZINES
The weekly *Bulletin* is Australia's answer to *Time* and *Newsweek*.

MEDICAL TREATMENT
● Doctors and dentists are readily available and there are many medical centres where appointments are not necessary.
● Hotels will help you locate a doctor.
● Medical, dental and ambulance services are excellent, but costly.
● British, New Zealand and some other nationals are entitled to 'immediate necessary treatment' under a reciprocal agreement but health insurance is still advisable. Dental services are not included.

MEDICINES
Visitors are permitted to bring prescribed medication in reasonable amounts. Bring your prescription and leave medications in their original containers to avoid problems at customs. Most prescription drugs are widely available.

RADIO
Melbourne has 15 major stations, ranging from FM rock music broadcasters such as Triple J-FM and Triple M-FM to the Australian Broadcasting Corporation's (ABC) Radio National and 3LO. There are also many AM music, chat and news stations.

TELEPHONES
● Public telephones are found at phone booths, post offices, hotels, petrol stations, shops, railway and bus stations, and cafés.
● Local calls cost 50¢ for unlimited time.
● Long-distance calls within Australia, known as STD calls, vary considerably in price, but you should have a good supply of 50¢, A$1 and A$2coins. Calls are cheaper after 6pm and on weekends.
● ☎ 12550 for operator assistance.
● ☎ 0011 for bookings and reverse-charge calls.

TOURIST INFORMATION
● Tourism Victoria
☎ 132 842
● City of Melbourne
☎ 9658 9658 🕐 Mon–Fri 9–5. Covers a range of accommodation.
● City Experience Centre
✉ Corner of Collins and Swanston streets ☎ 9658 9955. Features interactive tourist information about sightseeing.

PLACES OF WORSHIP
● Anglican: St. Paul's Cathedral ✉ Corner of Swanston and Flinders streets ☎ 9650 3791
● Roman Catholic: St. Patrick's Cathedral ✉ Cathedral Place ☎ 962 22336
● Baptist ✉ 174 Collins Street ☎ 9650 1801
● Orthodox Jewish: East Melbourne Synagogue ✉ 488 Albert Street, East Melbourne ☎ 9962 1372
● Buddhist: Buddhist Centre ☎ 9380 4303
● Muslim: City Mosque ✉ 66 Jeffcott Street, West Melbourne ☎ 9328 2067
● Uniting Church: St. Michael's ✉ 120 Collins Street ☎ 9545 1206

POST OFFICES AND POSTAGE

● Post offices are generally open Mon–Fri 9–5. Melbourne General Post Office hours are Mon–Fri 8.15–5.30, Sat 8.30–noon.
● Larger post offices sell airmails, and provide fax and e-mail facilities.
● Stamps can also be purchased in some hotels and from some newsagents and souvenir shops.

SENSIBLE PRECAUTIONS

● If you experience a theft or any other incident, report it to your hotel and to the police. If your travellers' cheques are stolen, advise the relevant organization.
● It is safe to drink tap water.
● The only medical problems you are likely to experience are sunburn and mosquito bites.
● For sun protection, make sure you have good supplies of SPF 15+ block, and wear sunglasses, a hat and long sleeves if you burn easily.
● Dangerous currents can cause problems in the sea in summer. Swim only at beaches with lifeguards, swim between the flags and observe any posted warnings.
● If you undertake long hikes, let someone know of your expected return time.

● Phonecards come in values of A\$5, A\$10 or A\$20; credit cards can also be used from some phones.
● International calls, known as ISD calls, can be made from your hotel and certain public telephones by dialing ☎ 0011, followed by the country codes: UK 44; US and Canada 1; France 33; Germany 49. For international enquiries ☎ 1255. To book an operator-connected call ☎ 12550.
● To call a Melbourne or Victoria number from outside the state, use the prefix 03. Calls from within the state require no prefix.

TELEVISION
● ABC (Australian Broadcasting Corporation) Channel 2 has no commercials.
● Melbourne has four commercial stations: Channels 7, 9, 10 and SBS (Special Broadcasting Service).
● Cable and satellite services are available in most major hotels.

TOILETS
Access to free public toilets can be found in parks, public places, galleries, museums, department stores and also in bus and railway stations. Most hotels will allow you to use their facilities.

VISITORS WITH DISABILITIES
People with mobility related impairments have a number of options for getting around in Melbourne. Many taxis have wheelchair access and the more modern trams and buses have wheelchair access and special seating. There are a number of accessible toilets, which meet current Australian Standards. Many attractions and sporting venues accommodate visitors with mobility related impairments. All parks provide wheelchair accessible paths and some also have accessible toilets.

More details can be found on the Visit Melbourne website: www.visitmelbourne.com under the 'Travel Info' menu.

Language

Most people understand the greeting 'G'day' as being Australian slang for 'hello'. But there are lots of other weird words and phrases that you're likely to encounter on a trip to Australia or when talking with the locals. Australians sometimes say several words as one 'waddayareckon' ('what do you reckon?') and 'owyagoin' ('how are you going?'). This can be confusing, but you will soon get used to it. Listed here are the meanings of some of the words and phrases you're most likely to hear.

AUSSIE ENGLISH

ankle biter	*small or young child*
arvo	*afternoon*
barney	*argument, fight*
big smoke	*the city*
bloke	*man*
bonza	*excellent, attractive*
bush	*the country*
chinwag	*chat, conversation*
cobber	*mate, friend*
dag	*person with little dress sense, uncouth*
drongo	*slow-witted person*
dunny	*outside toilet*
fair dinkum	*real, genuine, true*
full as a boot	*intoxicated*
get stuffed	*go away*
hard yakka	*hard work*
knock off	*to steal something, a counterfeit product*
larrikin	*lout, mischievous*
pommie	*English person*
rack off	*go away, get lost*
sheila	*girl, woman*
skite	*boast, brag*
slab	*carton of 24 beer cans*
struth!	*exclamation of surprise*
stubby	*small bottle of beer*
sunnies	*pair of sunglasses*
tee up	*to organize something*
tinnie	*can of beer*
true blue	*genuine*
tucker	*food*
yarn	*story*
yonks	*long period of time*

Timeline

ABORIGINAL PRESENCE

The Aboriginal people of the Port Phillip area lived in harmony with nature and by their traditional means for thousands of years before European settlement. The nearly 40 different tribal groups throughout present-day Victoria were descendants of people who made their way to the Australian mainland from Southeast Asia up to 60,000 years ago, and led a semi-nomadic existence. Hunting and gathering for sustenance, the people were bonded to their surroundings by a complex system of spiritual beliefs and their lives were governed by cultural codes handed down through the generations.

From left to right: Captain James Cook (1728–1779); early Aboriginal people; gold nuggets, panned during the Klondike gold rush; Old Parliament House; Quantas, the national airline of Australia

40,000–60,000 years ago
Aboriginal people arrive from Southeast Asia.

1770 English navigator Captain James Cook and the crew of the *Endeavour* arrive in Botany Bay, near the present location of Sydney.

1787 The First Fleet departs from Portsmouth, England. The 11 ships carry 1,400 people, comprising 756 convicts and a contingent of 644 soldiers.

1803 The British send ships to Port Phillip Bay to prevent French settlement.

1835 John Batman buys land around Port Phillip Bay from the Aboriginal people. Two years later, the site is renamed Melbourne, after the British Prime Minister.

1851 Gold is discovered near Ballarat. People flock from all over the world and Melbourne's population multiplies rapidly. The colony of Victoria separates from New South Wales.

1860s As Melbourne prospers, the foundations are laid for many grand buildings.

1861 The first Melbourne Cup is run.

1883 The first railway service begins between Melbourne and Sydney.

1890s Economic depression ends boom times for the country.

SPIRIT OF TASMANIA

1901 The Commonwealth of Australia is proclaimed, joining the six Australian colonies into a federation; the first Commonwealth Parliament opens in Melbourne.

1918 World War I ends. Sixty thousand Australians have died.

1927 Federal Parliament opens in Canberra.

1929 The Great Depression begins.

1934 Australia's national airline, Qantas, begins regular flights from Sydney to London.

1939 Black Friday bush fires kill 71 people in Victoria.

1939–45 Australian troops fight overseas during World War II, with over 35,000 war deaths.

1956 First television broadcast in Melbourne. The city hosts the XVI Olympiad.

1972 Australia's involvement in Vietnam ends, with 496 servicemen killed.

1994 Native Title Bill becomes law.

1999 Australia votes against becoming a republic.

2007 Prime Minister John Howard's 11-year reign comes to an end.

BOOM OR BUST

From the time of the gold rush onwards, and culminating in the Great Exhibition of 1888, the city of Melbourne enjoyed boom times created by the state's enormous mineral wealth. However, the bubble burst in the 1890s and the period of great economic depression that followed ruined numerous speculators and brought great hardship to many.

Index

CITYPACK TOP 25
Melbourne

WRITTEN BY Rod Ritchie
ADDITIONAL WRITING Julie Walkden
COVER DESIGN AND DESIGN WORK Jacqueline Bailey
INDEXER Marie Lorimer
IMAGE RETOUCHING AND REPRO Michael Moody, Sarah Montgomery
EDITORIAL MANAGEMENT Apostrophe S Limited
SERIES EDITOR Marie-Claire Jefferies

First published 2001
New edition 2008
Reprinted February 2010 and May 2011

Colour separation by Keenes, UK
Printed and bound by Leo Paper Products, China

A CIP catalogue record for this book is available from the British Library.

ISBN 978-0-7495-5703-4

Published by AA Publishing, a trading name of AA Media Limited, whose registered office is Fanum House, Basing View, Basingstoke, Hampshire RG21 4EA. Registered number 06112600.

A04737
Mapping in this title produced from map data supplied by Global Mapping, Brackley, UK. Copyright © Global Mapping/Meridian Maps
Transport map © Communicarta Ltd, UK

The Automobile Association wishes to thank the following photographers, companies and picture libraries for their assistance in the preparation of this book.

Abbreviations for the picture credits are as follows – (t) top; (b) bottom; (c) centre; (l) left; (r) right; (AA) AA World Travel Library.

Front cover Peter Dunphy/Tourism Victoria 1063708P800; **back cover (i)** AA/B Bachman 00203577; **(ii)** AA/C Sawyer 00156083; **(iii)** AA/B Bachman 00203571; **(iv)** AA/B Bachman 00155803; **1** AA/B Bachman; **2–18t** AA/B Bachman; **4** AA/B Bachman; **5** AA/B Bachman; **6cl** AA/B Bachman; **6cr** AA/B Bachman; **6bl** AA/B Bachman; **6bc** AA/J Freeman; **6br** Peter Dunphy/Tourism Victoria; **7cl** AA/C Sawyer; **7cc** Tim Webster/Tourism Victoria; **7cr** AA/B Bachman; **7bl** AA/B Bachman; **7bc** Peter Dunphy/Tourism Victoria; **7br** Peter Dunphy/Tourism Victoria; **10tr** AA/B Bachman; **10tcr** AA/B Bachman; **10/11** Photodisc; **10br** Photodisc; **11tl** AA/B Bachman; **11tcl** AA/B Bachman; **11bl** Peter Dunphy/Tourism Victoria; **13t** AA/B Bachman; **13c** AA/B Bachman; **13b** AA/B Bachman; **14tr** AA/B Bachman; **14tcr** AA/B Bachman; **14bcr** Photodisc; **14br** AA/B Bachman; **15b** AA/B Bachman; **16tr** AA/T Harris; **16tcr** Tourism Victoria; **16bcr** Photodisc; **16br** Peter Dunphy/Tourism Victoria; **17tl** Bindi Cole – Snap Happy/Tourism Victoria; **17tcl** Mark Chew/Tourism Victoria; **17bcl** AA/C Sawyer; **17bl** Melbourne Planetarium, Scienceworks; **18tr** Peter Dunphy/Tourism Victoria; **18tcr** AA/B Bachman; **18bcr** Peter Dunphy/Tourism Victoria; **18br** AA/B Bachman; **19(i)** AA/B Bachman; **19(ii)** AA/B Bachman; **19(iii)** Gavin Hansford/Tourism Victoria; **19(iv)** AA/B Bachman; **19(v)** AA/B Bachman; **19(vi)** AA/B Bachman; **20/21** Peter Dunphy/Tourism Victoria; **24tl** AA/B Bachman; **24tr** David Hannah/Tourism Victoria; **25tl** Gavin Hansford/Tourism Victoria; **25tr** AA/B Bachman; **26** AA/B Bachman; **27tl** AA/B Bachman; **27tc** AA/B Bachman; **27tr** AA/B Bachman; **28tl** National Trust of Australia (Victoria); **28tc** National Trust of Australia (Victoria); **28tr** National Trust of Australia (Victoria); **29** National Trust of Australia (Victoria); **30–31t** AA/B Bachman; **30bl** Media Unit – Tourism Victoria; **30br** AA/B Bachman; **31b** AA/B Bachman; **32** AA/B Bachman; **33t** AA/B Bachman; **34–35t** Mark Chew/Tourism Victoria; **36–37t** Tourism Victoria; **37c** Mark Chew/Tourism Victoria; **38t** Mark Chew/Tourism Victoria; **39** Peter Dunphy/Tourism Victoria; **42l** Peter Dunphy/Tourism Victoria; **42/43t** AA/B Bachman; **42/43c** Peter Dunphy/Tourism Victoria; **43c** Mark Chew/Tourism Victoria; **44tl** Peter Dunphy/Tourism Victoria; **44tr** Peter Dunphy/Tourism Victoria; **45tl** Immigration Museum; **45tr** AA/B Bachman; **46l** AA/B Bachman; **46/47t** AA/B Bachman; **46/47c** AA/B Bachman; **48tl** James Lauritz/Tourism Victoria; **48tr** Peter Dunphy/Tourism Victoria; **49** AA/B Bachman; **50t** AA/B Bachman; **50bl** AA/B Bachman; **50br** Enzo Amato/Tourism Victoria; **51t** Mark Chew/Tourism Victoria; **51c** Tourism Victoria; **52** Mark Chew/Tourism Victoria; **53** Peter Dunphy/Tourism Victoria; **56tl** Peter Dunphy/Tourism Victoria; **56tr** Tourism Victoria; **57tl** Peter Dunphy/Tourism Victoria; **57tr** Peter Dunphy/Tourism Victoria; **58** Peter Dunphy/Tourism Victoria; **59t** AA/A Baker; **59cl** Peter Dunphy/Tourism Victoria; **59cr** Peter Dunphy/Tourism Victoria; **60l** Royal Botanic Gardens; **60/61t** AA/B Bachman; **60/61cl** AA/J Wood; **61cl** AA/B Bachman; **61cr** Royal Botanic Gardens; **62tl** Peter Dunphy/Tourism Victoria; **62tc** AA/B Bachman; **62tr** AA/B Bachman; **63t** AA/B Bachman; **63bl** AA/B Bachman; **63br** Mark Chew/Tourism Victoria; **64t** AA/B Bachman; **65–66t** Mark Chew/Tourism Victoria; **67t** Tourism Victoria; **68t** Mark Chew/Tourism Victoria; **69** AA/B Bachman; **72** Gavin Hansford/Tourism Victoria; **73tl** Tourism Victoria; **73tr** AA/A Baker; **74tl** David Hannah/Tourism Victoria; **74tr** AA/B Bachman; **75t** AA/B Bachman; **75b** AA/B Bachman; **76** Photodisc; **77t** Mark Chew/Tourism Victoria; **77c** Tourism Victoria; **78t** Mark Chew/Tourism Victoria; **79** AA/B Bachman; **82tl** White Studios/ Tourism Victoria; **82tr** Tim Webster/Tourism Victoria; **83tl** AA/B Bachman; **83tr** AA/B Bachman; **84tl** AA/B Bachman; **84tr** AA/B Bachman; **85tl** AA/B Bachman; **85tc** AA/B Bachman; **85tr** AA/B Bachman; **86t** AA/B Bachman; **86bl** AA/B Bachman; **86br** AA/B Bachman; **87t** AA/B Bachman; **88t** Mark Chew/Tourism Victoria; **89t** Tourism Victoria; **90t** Mark Chew/Tourism Victoria; **91** AA/B Bachman; **94tl** Heide Museum of Modern Art Collection, Commissioned through the Heide Foundation with significant assistance from Lindsay and Paula Fox 2005, Photographer: John Gollings 2006, © Inge King & John Gollings; **94tr** Architect: O'Connor + Houle Architecture, Photographer: John Gollings 2006, © John Gollings; **95tl** AA/B Bachman; **95tr** National Trust of Australia (Victoria); **96tl** Scienceworks; **96tr** Scienceworks; **97** AA/B Bachman; **98t** AA/B Bachman; **98bl** AA/B Bachman; **98br** AA/B Bachman; **99t** AA/B Bachman; **100** AA/B Bachman; **101–102t** AA/B Bachman; **103t** Mark Chew/Tourism Victoria; **104t** Tourism Victoria; **105** AA/B Bachman; **106t** Mark Chew/Tourism Victoria; **107** Peter Dunphy/Tourism Victoria; **108–112t** AA/C Sawyer; **108tr** Stockbyte Royalty Free; **108tcr** Stockbyte Royalty Free; **108bcr** Mark Chew/Tourism Victoria; **108br** AA/B Bachman; **113** AA/B Bachman; **114–125t** AA/B Bachman; **120** MRI Bankers' Guide to Foreign Currency, Houston, USA; **123** AA/C Osborne; **124bl** AA; **124bc** AA; **124br** AA/C Coe; **125bl** AA/A Baker; **125br** AA/M Langford

Every effort has been made to trace the copyright holders, and we apologise in advance for any unintentional omissions or errors. We would be pleased to apply any corrections in any following edition of this publication.